# *POETIC VOYAGES GLOUCESTERSHIRE*

Edited by Allison Dowse

First published in Great Britain in 2001 by
*YOUNG WRITERS*
Remus House,
Coltsfoot Drive,
Peterborough, PE2 9JX
Telephone (01733) 890066

All Rights Reserved

*Copyright Contributors 2001*

HB ISBN 0 75433 182 2
SB ISBN 0 75433 183 0

## *Foreword*

Young Writers was established in 1991 with the aim to promote creative writing in children, to make reading and writing poetry fun.

This year once again, proved to be a tremendous success with over 88,000 entries received nationwide.

The Poetic Voyages competition has shown us the high standard of work and effort that children are capable of today. It is a reflection of the teaching skills in schools, the enthusiasm and creativity they have injected into their pupils shines clearly within this anthology.

The task of selecting poems was therefore a difficult one but nevertheless, an enjoyable experience. We hope you are as pleased with the final selection in *Poetic Voyages Gloucestershire* as we are.

# CONTENTS

| | | |
|---|---|---|
| | Victoria Ellis | 1 |
| Blakeney CP School | | |
| | Louise Anne Morton | 1 |
| | Katy Chivers | 2 |
| | Liam White | 2 |
| | Joe Young | 3 |
| | William Harris | 3 |
| | Robbie Fennell | 4 |
| | Aaron Davis | 4 |
| | Tara Parry | 5 |
| | Jodie Dawson | 5 |
| | Oliver Walter | 6 |
| | Ross Cecil | 6 |
| | Sophie Jarvis | 7 |
| | Gareth Jones | 7 |
| | Ross Johnson | 8 |
| Chalford Hill Primary School | | |
| | Tom Horrell | 8 |
| | Daniel Mitchell | 9 |
| | Emily Tibbs-Hall | 9 |
| | Robyn Perry | 9 |
| | Adam Gibbons | 10 |
| | Tommy Woods | 10 |
| | Katie-Anne Salter | 10 |
| | Max Findlay | 11 |
| | Megan Shepherd | 11 |
| | Ben Lucas | 11 |
| | Daisy Bateman | 12 |
| | Alistair Duncan Gilchrist | 12 |
| | Kristian Richings | 12 |
| | James Chandler | 13 |
| | Chris Brain | 13 |

Charlton Kings Junior School
| | |
|---|---|
| Adele Toyne | 13 |
| William Wilkinson | 14 |
| Rebecca Jones | 14 |
| Bryony Baker | 15 |

Hesters Way Junior School
| | |
|---|---|
| Jamie Jerkovic | 15 |
| Harinda Ferguson | 16 |
| Asa Hearn | 16 |
| Daniel Belcher | 17 |
| Tom Tucker | 18 |
| Mellissa Moxey | 18 |

Hopes Hill Primary School
| | |
|---|---|
| Henry Gardner | 19 |
| Michelle Harding | 19 |
| Thomas Penson | 19 |
| Joey Collins | 20 |
| Lauren Barnes | 20 |
| Mark Brooks | 21 |
| Simon Read | 21 |
| Araminta McShee | 22 |
| Rachel Brooks | 22 |
| Joanna Priest | 23 |
| Daniel McShee | 23 |

Kingswood Primary School
| | |
|---|---|
| Lauren Workman | 23 |
| Kim Terrett | 24 |
| Tash Fry | 24 |
| Holly Walter | 25 |
| Ellen Devine | 26 |
| George Williams | 27 |
| Mark Robertson | 28 |
| Megan Harrison | 28 |
| Sam Adams | 29 |

| | |
|---|---|
| Abigail Beswick | 30 |
| **Leighterton Primary School** | |
| Christie Jarrett | 30 |
| Robert Lord | 31 |
| Harriet Wallington | 32 |
| Sarah Mould | 32 |
| Josua Tuck | 33 |
| **Leonard Stanley CE Primary School** | |
| Callum Watson-Kemp | 34 |
| Jessica Gibson | 34 |
| Jemma Field | 34 |
| Amy Matthews | 35 |
| Amelia Glassonbury | 35 |
| Emma Fitter | 36 |
| Rachel Bayliss | 36 |
| Lauren Oakes | 37 |
| Kerry Prictor | 37 |
| Emma Stephens | 38 |
| Elliot Rees | 38 |
| Alexandra Bayliss | 39 |
| Rory Birch | 39 |
| **Longborough CE Primary School** | |
| Timothy Williams-Ellis | 40 |
| Amy Townsend | 40 |
| Joseph Deane | 41 |
| Jessica Murray | 41 |
| Joe Nott | 42 |
| Alexander Tweddell | 42 |
| Kristie Ellery | 43 |
| Louise Griffiths | 43 |
| Charlotte Townsend | 44 |
| Chris Burger | 44 |
| Nathan Simpson | 45 |
| Laura McPherson | 45 |

Longlevens Junior School
|  |  |
|---|---|
| Daniel Wilcox | 46 |
| Mark Creese | 46 |
| Lucy Henderson | 47 |
| Georgina Marfell | 47 |
| Ben Kirby | 48 |
| Laurence Mezo | 48 |
| Martin Feighan | 49 |
| Yasmin Kadodia | 50 |
| Daniel Dixon | 50 |
| Samuel English | 51 |
| Joanna Steel | 52 |
| Craig James | 52 |
| Craig Jones | 53 |

Lydney CE Primary School
|  |  |
|---|---|
| Joseph Legge | 54 |
| Tessa Jones | 55 |
| Jessica King | 56 |
| Ashley Edwards, Shane Symonds & Andrew Dodds | 57 |
| Niall Walker & Lloyd Barker | 58 |
| Emma Fletcher | 59 |
| Thomas Sollis | 60 |
| Katie Williams | 61 |
| Tiannie Bowery & Danielle Watkins | 62 |
| Gabrielle Olley | 63 |

North Cerney CE Primary School
|  |  |
|---|---|
| Samantha Cairns, Rebecca Young & Holly Tarrant | 63 |
| Joseph Johnson | 64 |
| Linden Moy, Sam Greenwood & Christopher Horton | 64 |
| Isabella Horton | 65 |
| Thomas Franklin & Jack Hale | 65 |
| Luke Ellis | 66 |
| Lianne Katie Weeks | 66 |

| | |
|---|---|
| James Tarrant | 67 |
| William Seymour, Joe Walker | |
|     & Nicholas Holder | 67 |
| Joe Johnson | 68 |
| Ben Barton, William Seymour | |
|     & Robert Gardiner | 69 |

**Northleach CE Primary School**

| | |
|---|---|
| Victoria Turner | 69 |
| Ayla Kelly | 70 |
| Charlotte Fothergill | 70 |
| James Clayton | 71 |
| Alexandra Goddard | 71 |
| Sarah-Louise Morgan | 72 |
| Jasmine Burns | 72 |
| Joe Sellwood | 73 |
| Samantha Norman | 73 |
| Charles Meacher | 74 |
| Amy Edwards | 74 |
| Bradley Spedding | 75 |
| Imogen McConnon | 75 |
| Simon Page | 76 |
| Max Yates | 76 |
| Amy Hubbard | 77 |
| Joanna Rainey | 77 |

**St David's Primary School, Moreton-in-Marsh**

| | |
|---|---|
| Natasha Didcote | 77 |
| Daniel Abrahams | 78 |
| Becky Udell | 79 |
| Emma Norton | 80 |
| Alice Byrne | 80 |
| Samuel Evans | 81 |
| Sam Turner | 81 |
| Katie Foylan | 82 |
| Esme Baggott | 82 |
| Leigh-Anne Woskett | 83 |
| Kate Burrows | 83 |

| | |
|---|---|
| David Groom | 84 |
| Leo Newman | 84 |
| Jake Wright | 85 |
| Daisy Perry | 85 |
| Niall Arthurs | 86 |
| James Henshaw | 86 |
| Jodie Harrison | 87 |
| Thomas Barton | 88 |
| Chelsea Dyer | 88 |
| Alexandra Parker | 89 |
| Jennifer Rolton | 89 |

St John's Primary School, Cheltenham

| | |
|---|---|
| Sam Reeves | 89 |
| Charlotte Cambray | 90 |
| Carrie Knight | 90 |
| Sam Thacker | 91 |
| Laurie Wright | 92 |
| Micky Gibbard | 92 |
| Leah Evans | 93 |
| James Martin | 93 |

St Lawrence Primary School, Lechlade

| | |
|---|---|
| Peter Williams | 94 |
| Stacey Carter | 94 |
| Emma Cashin | 95 |
| Laura Jones | 96 |
| Jamie Tanner | 96 |
| Vicky Challoner | 97 |
| Megan Kennedy | 98 |
| Geoffrey Harding | 98 |
| James Somers | 99 |
| Rachel Leonard | 100 |
| Kien Lieu | 100 |
| Christopher Carroll | 101 |
| Joshua Nicoll | 102 |
| Piers Powers | 102 |
| Kieran Gandhi | 103 |

St Paul's CE Primary School, Gloucester
| | |
|---|---|
| Morwenna Bennett | 104 |
| Edward Hood | 104 |
| Candice Williams | 105 |
| Sam Azmayesh | 106 |
| Michael Witts | 106 |
| Ryan Faherty | 107 |
| Stephen Hood | 107 |
| Christina Read | 108 |
| Joe Young | 108 |
| Rachel Bown | 109 |
| Tamara Birch | 109 |
| Jamie Douglas | 110 |
| Ryan Barnard | 110 |
| Hannah Blackwell | 111 |
| Jack Parry | 111 |
| Jade Barnes | 112 |
| Jamie Allen | 112 |

Slimbridge Primary School
| | |
|---|---|
| Hannah Price | 113 |
| Ricky Hewer | 113 |
| Harriet Osborne | 114 |
| Abigail Poulton | 114 |
| Hannah Brown | 115 |
| James Whetherly | 116 |
| Andrew Foster | 116 |
| Simeon Koole | 117 |
| Sophie Tremlin | 118 |
| Hannah Koole | 118 |
| Natasha Frewer | 119 |
| Ceri Wills | 120 |
| Helen Hanstock | 121 |
| Katie Frewer | 122 |

Swindon Village Primary School
| | |
|---|---|
| Robert Cullimore & Owain McFarlane | 122 |
| Charlotte Brewer | 123 |

| | |
|---|---|
| Simon Langley | 124 |
| Peter Griffiths | 124 |
| Dhru Mistry | 125 |
| Shona Wilson | 125 |
| Matthew Evans | 125 |
| Debbie Lloyd | 126 |
| Charlotte Morris | 126 |
| Kelsey Lonergan | 127 |
| Tamara Morgan | 127 |
| Steven Wootten | 128 |
| Nathan Roberts | 128 |
| Jack Stanley | 129 |
| Milli Cornock | 129 |
| Matthew Adair | 130 |
| Molly Chapman | 130 |
| Adam Knowles | 131 |
| Janine Irwin | 132 |
| Tanya Hopson | 132 |
| Louise Rogers | 133 |

The Moat Junior School

| | |
|---|---|
| Thomas Warnes | 133 |
| Zak Hayes | 134 |
| Kelsey Goodwin | 134 |
| Danielle Thornhill | 135 |
| Mark Sysum | 135 |
| Nina Foot | 136 |
| Ross Farrell | 136 |
| Kieron Fitzgibbon | 137 |
| Rosanne Dowding | 137 |
| Kelly Miles | 138 |
| Shaun Huntley | 138 |
| Christopher Partlett | 139 |
| Samantha Turner | 139 |
| Daniel Wright | 140 |
| Samuel Critchley | 140 |
| Zoe Carter | 141 |
| Charlotte Owen | 141 |

| | |
|---|---|
| Emma Willetts | 142 |
| Tyrell Williams | 142 |
| Lee Gordon | 143 |
| Josh Rogers | 143 |
| Stephen Fitt | 144 |
| Stacey Lee | 144 |
| Class 3B | 145 |
| Elisha Blackwood | 145 |
| David Black | 146 |
| Steven Partlett | 146 |
| Holli Thompson | 147 |
| David Clarke | 147 |
| Vicky Scott | 148 |
| Josh Hawkins | 148 |
| Class 3A | 149 |
| Ashley Caine | 149 |
| Danielle Dillon | 150 |
| Sam Myatt | 150 |
| Giorgette Bendle | 151 |
| Jade Stevens | 151 |
| Scott Franklin | 152 |
| Ben Hooper | 152 |
| Sean Johnson | 153 |
| Michelle Blackford | 153 |
| Michael MacDonald | 154 |
| Anne Carpenter | 154 |
| Josh Patel | 154 |
| Karina Clutterbuck | 155 |
| Daniel Vijay | 155 |
| Sam Vijay | 156 |
| Michaela Marsh | 156 |
| Natasha Ogden | 157 |
| Jordan Bombera | 157 |
| Larissa Woodhouse | 158 |
| Joanna Alice Clarke | 158 |

The Richard Pate School
- Dominic Lane — 159
- Michael Greene — 160
- Charlotte Morton — 160
- Imogen Ryley — 161
- Jack Sim — 162
- Shona Pratt — 162
- Amanda Ripley — 163
- Francesca White — 164
- David Hackett — 164
- Harry Young — 165
- Emily Field — 165
- Amelia Peace — 166
- Hannah Barraclough — 166

Tewkesbury CE Primary School
- Tim Pettitt — 167
- Lucy Paginton — 168
- Emma King — 168
- Shardai Thomas — 169
- Daniel Defty — 169
- Jessica Courtney — 170
- Kelly Wynne — 170
- Ben Torr — 171
- Gemma Newman — 172
- Sam Cotton — 172
- Fahad Nazmul — 173
- Jamie Powell — 173
- Charlotte Hamilton — 174
- Sam Devine — 174
- Stacey Baldwin — 175
- Christopher Callow — 175
- Callum Kerr — 176
- Abigail Bullingham — 177
- Lee Phillips — 178
- Rebecca Ricketts — 178
- Rebecca Nash — 179
- William Devine — 179

| | |
|---|---|
| Rachel Gibbs | 180 |
| Emily Blackwell | 180 |
| John Vincent | 181 |
| Chris Tarling | 181 |
| Rhys Bestwick | 182 |
| Rebecca Ramplin | 182 |
| Ian Vedmore | 183 |
| Ashleigh Hesslewood | 184 |
| Georgina Harvey | 185 |

Toddington Primary School

| | |
|---|---|
| Charlotte Sherwood | 185 |

Tuffley Primary School

| | |
|---|---|
| Paula Thomas | 186 |
| Stacey Davis | 186 |
| Daniel Anderson | 187 |
| Daniel Brookes | 187 |
| Jade Ryan | 188 |
| Eddie Carter | 188 |
| Leigh Dangerfield | 189 |
| Leah Davis | 189 |
| King Yip | 190 |
| Laura Barnard | 190 |
| Shaun Beresford | 191 |
| Natalie Beard | 191 |
| Kerry Brookes | 191 |
| Jake Dabbs | 192 |
| Katherine Anderson | 193 |

*The Poems*

## THE WEATHER

Rainy days,
Spoil our plays.
Sun comes out,
Give a shout.
We can play,
Rest of the day.
That'll be fun,
Play in the sun!

*Victoria Ellis (10)*


## ANIMALS

Why do wolves howl at night?
Because they're trying to seek out friends
from a long, misty distance.

Why do puppies yelp?
Because they have to go in the
bubbly wet bath.

Why do glow-worms glow?
To light the darkened way of others
creeping in the mist.

Why do mice gnaw?
To build a cosy warm bed under the
dusty, rotten floorboards under the house.

Why are unicorns a myth?
Because they live in leprechaun land,
far, far away in the clouds where no one can find them.

*Louise Anne Morton (10)*
*Blakeney CP School*

## PEOPLE AND ANIMALS

Why do animals make their own noise?
So they can communicate with the wind as it whistles.
Why do people live in houses?
So the rain won't hit them like bombs attacking.
Why do people take a bath?
So the morning smells fresh.
Why do people have to read?
To get around.
How?
You can read the pathway.
Why?
The pathway leads to a new world.

*Katy Chivers (9)*
*Blakeney CP School*




## THE WEATHER

Why does the wind blow?
There is nowhere for it to depart.
How do clouds develop?
From the mist on a foggy day.
When does rain fall?
When the earth is dehydrated.
When does the rain stop?
When the sky is as dry as a desert.

*Liam White (10)*
*Blakeney CP School*

## TIME

What is time?
The never-ending passage floating through life.

Where does time come from?
Where nobody has ever been.

Who invented time?
The bitter blowing winds of nature.

What does time do?
Rock back and forth, waiting for it to age.

How long has time been here?
Before anything had been awakened.

When will time end?
When the entire universe is no more.

*Joe Young (11)*
*Blakeney CP School*


## THE WEATHER

Why does the wind blow?
So the sky can breathe.

How do the snowflakes fall ?
From the ice-cold mountains.

Where do the flames come from?
A dragon's lava pit.

*William Harris (10)*
*Blakeney CP School*

## THE WEATHER

Why does the sun shine?
To cheer up your miserable day.

Where does lightning come from?
From the deep reaches of the dark universe.

Why does lightning strike?
Because it's filled with red-hot anger.

Why does the wind blow?
To cool down the boiling hot world.

When does the rain stop?
When it runs into the dark, murky sewers.

Where does the rain come from?
The deep, salty, blue oceans.

*Robbie Fennell (10)*
*Blakeney CP School*


## THE WEATHER

Why does the wind blow?
It hasn't found anywhere to depart.
Why does the rain downswing?
To aggravate everyone.
Why does it snow?
It has no time to stand and look fixedly.
When does the downpour stop?
When the skies are dehydrated.
Does the weather ever stop?
No, it has to depart.
Where does the lightning come from?
From electricity bursting from the sky above.

*Aaron Davis (9)*
*Blakeney CP School*

## THE SEA

Why is the sea salty?
A clumsy man dropped a bag of
forever salt into the horrific sea.
Why is the sea blue?
It flows peacefully with the calm colour.
Why are there waves?
The stormy weather vigorously blows the sea about.
Why is the sea made up of water?
Someone accidentally left the tap running.
Why doesn't the sea evaporate?
There is too much of it to let it waste away.
Why do we have lots of seas?
For the creatures to swim beyond.

*Tara Parry (10)*
**Blakeney CP School**


## THE GRASS

Why is the grass green?
An artist was painting and spilt green paint.
Why does the grass grow?
It feeds on disgusting insects.
Why don't we eat grass?
There would be no food for the animals.
Why do we cut the grass?
It would invade our homes if we didn't.
Why can't we change the colour of the grass?
The paint is everlasting.
Why is grass called grass?
It was made to be part of the Earth.

*Jodie Dawson (11)*
**Blakeney CP School**

## THE WEATHER

Where does snow come from?
It comes from the icy depths of the North Pole.

Why does the wind blow?
God is howling in rage from the sky.

When does it rain?
When the sky is ripped open by a gigantic dinosaur.

Why does lightning never hit in the same place twice?
It is being pushed by a monster made of electricity.

Why does the sun shine?
Because everyone in the world is having fun playing together.

Why is snow cold?
It comes from a freezing hole in space.

*Oliver Walter (10)*
*Blakeney CP School*




## THE WEATHER

Why does it snow?
So we can have a white Christmas.
Why does the wind blow?
So we won't suffer from the dreadful heat.
Where do the flames come from?
The dragon's lair.

*Ross Cecil (10)*
*Blakeney CP School*

## THE WORLD

What is really at the end of every rainbow?
    A new and positive world.
What is inside every happy child?
    A gleaming heart of gold.
Why is the world so far away from other planets?
    It is special.
Why do people scream and shout?
    To open up their true feelings from deep inside.
When do we really die?
    When the world turns cold and empty.
Who invented love?
    Everyone in this special world.
What surrounds every individual person?
    A loving and caring family.
What is the meaning of working together?
    Winning together.

*Sophie Jarvis (9)*
*Blakeney CP School*


## THE WEATHER

What is the wind?
The breathing of an historic dinosaur.
Where does the sun go at night?
Behind the rocky cliffs by the ocean.
Why does it always rain when you want to go out?
Because the universe is slashed open.
What is fog?
A dense layer of skin.

*Gareth Jones (10)*
*Blakeney CP School*

## THE WEATHER

Why does lightning strike?
It's filled with boiling, hot lava.

When does the rain stop?
When it hits the fertile soil.

Why does the sun shine?
It's overjoyed.

What is a tornado?
A never-ending black hole.

Why does the wind blow?
To cool down the hot world.

Where does the rainbow end?
At the bottom of the universe.

*Ross Johnson (10)*
*Blakeney CP School*


## DEATH

Death is gloomy blue,
It smells like dead rats
And tastes of poisonous frogs.
Death sounds like a squeal
And feels like a blood-soaked dagger.
Death lives in the heart of blood.

*Tom Horrell (9)*
*Chalford Hill Primary School*

## DEATH

Death is the colour of red
And smells like rotten skin.
It tastes like burning rubber
And sounds like a shotgun.
It feels like cold, damp wind
And it lives in a cellar.

***Daniel Mitchell (9)***
***Chalford Hill Primary School***

## HEALTH

Health is creamy blue
It smells like sweet tropical fruits
And tastes like white chocolate.
Health sounds like fun
And feels smooth.
Health lives in a garden.

***Emily Tibbs-Hall (9)***
***Chalford Hill Primary School***

## ANGER

Anger is dark brown
It smells like old fish
And tastes like mud.
Anger sounds restless
It feels like heat
And lives in the heart of a wall.

***Robyn Perry (9)***
***Chalford Hill Primary School***

## WAR

War is yellow and red
It smells like smoke
And it tastes like blood.
War sounds like a thunderstorm
And it feels like flaming skin.
It lives in a war field.

*Adam Gibbons (9)*
*Chalford Hill Primary School*

## DEATH

Death is blood-red
It smells like burning rubber
And tastes like sweltered coal.
Death sounds like screaming
And feels like scalding wax.
Death lives in your shadow.

*Tommy Woods (9)*
*Chalford Hill Primary School*

## HEALTH

Health is bright blue
It smells like strawberries.
Health tastes like grapes
It sounds like peace,
It feels great
And lives in the hospital.

*Katie-Anne Salter (9)*
*Chalford Hill Primary School*

## PAIN

Pain is the colour of blood-red
it smells like polluted air.
Pain tastes like burning rubber
it sounds like the screeching of a car as it skids out the way of a boy.
Pain feels like being beaten by a wrestler.
Pain lives in the depths of a volcano.

*Max Findlay (10)*
*Chalford Hill Primary School*


## FRIENDSHIP

Friendship is bright orange
It smells like sweets
And tastes like pizza.
Friendship sounds like a school in the summer
And feels like velvet.
Friendship lives in the sky.

*Megan Shepherd (9)*
*Chalford Hill Primary School*


## PEACE

Peace is a light blue
It smells like the summer air.
Peace tastes like peach
And sounds like birds singing.
Peace feels like cold wind
And it lives in the winter water.

*Ben Lucas (10)*
*Chalford Hill Primary School*

## CRUELTY

Cruelty is concrete grey
And smells like decay.
Cruelty tastes like cold Brussels sprouts
It smells like bullying
And feels like being helpless.
Cruelty lives at the bottom of the sea
In a dark, dark cave.

*Daisy Bateman (9)*
*Chalford Hill Primary School*


## WAR

War is brutally blue
it smells like a bad odour
and tastes like a hot meat.
War sounds like a bad battle
it feels like crashing axes.
War lives in killing blood.

*Alistair Duncan Gilchrist (10)*
*Chalford Hill Primary School*


## FRIENDSHIP

Friendship is bright orange
it smells like lovely ripe grapes
It tastes like luscious lime,
it sounds like laughter.
It feels warm and cosy inside
and lives in everyone.

*Kristian Richings (10)*
*Chalford Hill Primary School*

## FRIENDSHIP

Friendship is light blue
It smells like summer flowers
And tastes like juicy strawberries.
Friendship sounds like people singing happily
And feels like cuddly teddies.
Friendship lives in cosy, floating clouds.

*James Chandler (9)*
*Chalford Hill Primary School*

## WAR

War is brown,
it smells like blood
and tastes of flesh.
War sounds like pistols firing
it feels as if the world has ended.

*Chris Brain (9)*
*Chalford Hill Primary School*

## FAIRIES

My brother said they did not exist
Oh how, oh how he was wrong.
Fairies are dwelling in the garden
Oh how, oh how was he wrong.
I saw one so late in the night,
I saw them come out to play.
Small but quick, beautiful in the moonlight.
My brother said they did not exist
Oh how, oh how was he wrong.

*Adele Toyne (9)*
*Charlton Kings Junior School*

## THE TEACHERS' PARADISE

When I was lurking in the staffroom guess what I found . . .

Ten bottles of wine, white and sparkling,
Nine cans of cola, brown and fizzy,
Eight cups of coffee,
Seven bags of crisps, crunched on the sofa,
Six lollies, red, under the books,
Five bags of sugar in the cupboard
Four apples, juicy and ripe
Three boxes of chocolate, half-eaten from last week,
Two ice creams dripping on the floor
And guess what? One bowl of curry beans *uuurrgghh!*

***William Wilkinson (9)***
***Charlton Kings Junior School***


## AUTUMN LEAVES

When autumn comes and leaves turn brown
The cold wind blows and blows
Them down.

The gardener sweeps
A huge big pile
And lets them dry a little while.

A lighted match sets leaves alight
The leaves burn bright all through the night.

He goes inside and shuts the door
The leaves are gone forever more!

***Rebecca Jones (9)***
***Charlton Kings Junior School***

## MY STREET

'My street is not a noisy street.'
Say the scuttling squirrels, the singing birds
and the fluttering butterflies.

'My street is not a messy street.'
Say the green gardens, the colourful flowers
and the swaying trees.

'My street is not a busy street.'
Say the scattered conkers, the buzzing bees
and the blooming branches.

'My street is not a fast street.'
Say the grey roads, the playing children
and the sleeping policemen.

'My street is great!'
Says me.

*Bryony Baker (9)*
*Charlton Kings Junior School*


## THE MASSIVE SKYSCRAPER

The massive skyscraper built a couple of years ago,
An overpowering monster, huge . . .
like a volcano reaching the clouds,
like a giant touching the sky.
It makes me feel like an insect,
like a tiny greenfly that can't be seen.
The massive skyscraper
reminds us how small we are.

*Jamie Jerkovic (10)*
*Hesters Way Junior School*

## IT CAN'T BE A GHOST IT MUST BE MY EYES

A spirit glides through the empty hall
into the living room.
A spooky shadow trying to find its way
into the kitchen.
A sound of banging footsteps
make me cringe.
A shadow glides through
the moonlight.
It can't be a ghost, it must be my eyes!

As a strange mist floats through
the window,
A gust of wind and the door
is firmly shut.
The door was open then it
closed all by itself,
It can't be a ghost, it must be my eyes.

My mind is blank.
I can't remember turning
the light out.
The passageway is black as
the sky,
A bright flash through the window
Is it a ghost?
It must be my eyes.

*Harinda Ferguson (11)*
*Hesters Way Junior School*

## OUR WORLD

You can smell the sizzling burgers with melted cheese on the top,
The taste of a crispy hot dog after Manchester United beat Arsenal 3-0,
The touch of a dolphin when it is swimming in the sea,
The fantastic sound of a bird chirping in the morning,
A tiger in the middle of the African jungle, ready to pounce on his prey.

You can smell the fantastic aroma of a new book as it has just been opened,
The taste of a salted packet of crisps as it melts in your mouth,
The touch of a leather football as it falls out of your hands,
The crunching sound as I eat a piece of crunchy toast,
I can see the lovely fresh flowers as they let out their pollen.

*Asa Hearn (10)*
*Hesters Way Junior School*


## SPOOKS

The deserted cottage
Like a dark underground cave
Black, dusty, undiscovered,
Like a lowly spirit drifting around
Like he has been frightened
It feels like he's coming for me
Like a human trap in its cave.
The deserted cottage
It reminds us that we have got family.

The old house
It has been haunted for two years,
Small, old, weak,
Like a baby standing still
Like he's pointing to his bottle
It makes me feel very young.

The old house
The old house reminds us how young we are.

*Daniel Belcher (10)*
*Hesters Way Junior School*

## MANCHESTER UNITED FC VS WEST HAM UNITED FC

It was the big match,
Man U played West Ham on Sunday 28th at Old Trafford,
The fans were cheering for the 2pm kick-off,
In the FA Cup, fourth round.

The red and blue shirts came out of the tunnel,
Man U took the kick-off,
West Ham were pressurising them
Man U battled back to try and win the Cup.

West Ham took the kick-off for the second half
Kanoute passed the ball to Paulo DiCanio and 'Goal!'
West Ham had taken the lead, the crowd went wild.
Barthez ran up the pitch but the final whistle blew
West Ham had knocked Man U out of the Cup.

'The champions were out!'

*Tom Tucker (10)*
*Hesters Way Junior School*


## THE BEACH

As the sand runs through your fingers,
You can hear the waves crashing into each other,
Dolphins are speaking in their language under the deep blue sea,
The stars sparkling as they glide past the moon,
As the cockerel crows out at dawn the sun rises,
Seagulls flying across the sun.

*Mellissa Moxey (11)*
*Hesters Way Junior School*

## HORROR

Horror is grey, black and dark red
Horror smells like old mildew bread
Horror tastes like cold and ice
Horror sounds like lots of people screaming of murder
Horror feels like wind blowing down your neck
Horror lives in pain and suffering.

*Henry Gardner (10)*
*Hopes Hill Primary School*


## GUILT

Guilt is maroon
It smells like burnt rubber
Guilt tastes of mildew potatoes
It sounds like breaking glass
It feels like sharp thorns
Guilt lives in knots in your stomach.

*Michelle Harding (11)*
*Hopes Hill Primary School*


## TRUTH

Truth is yellow
It smells like the new bud of a rose
Truth tastes sweet or sour
It sounds like children playing
It feels sharp and smooth
Truth lives in your heart.

*Thomas Penson (9)*
*Hopes Hill Primary School*

## TOUCH

Touch!
(What can you feel?)
The prickles
of a hedgehog on a summer day.
The freezing snow
on the ground does lay.

Touch
(What can you feel?)
The cold ice
of a long icicle,
The leather ball
flying over the wall.

*Joey Collins (8)*
*Hopes Hill Primary School*


## TOUCH

Touch!
(What can you feel?)
The spikes
of a hedgehog in the dark, black night,
The silk of a fox coming into sight.

Touch!
(What can you feel?)
The fluffiness
of a newborn chick,
The hardness of a building brick.

*Lauren Barnes (8)*
*Hopes Hill Primary School*

## TOUCH

Touch!
(What can you feel?)
The sharp prickles
of a crawling hedgehog.
The feel of a rock like a wooden log.

Touch!
(What can you feel?)
The tickling
of a holly tree.
The touch of a fur and a boy called Lee.

***Mark Brooks (9)***
***Hopes Hill Primary School***


## TOUCH

*Touch*
What can you feel?
The fur
of a dog tickling me.
The sting of a stripy bumblebee.

*Touch*
What can you feel?
The slither
of a snake biting me,
the large golden door key.

***Simon Read (8)***
***Hopes Hill Primary School***

## WAR AND PEACE

*War*

War is a dirty red colour,
War smells like a mouldy egg.
War tastes like a bitter drink,
War sounds like crying pain.
War feels jagged and sharp,
War lives in distrustful hearts.

*Peace*

Peace is a light yellow colour,
Peace smells like a light floral fragrance.
Peace tastes like a ripe melon,
Peace sounds like a wind chime in a light wind.
Peace feels smooth like a pebble,
Peace lives in a child's heart.

***Araminta McShee (11)***
***Hopes Hill Primary School***


## EMPTINESS

Emptiness is black,
It smells like a burnt up car,
Emptiness tastes like crunchy
burnt sausages,
It sounds like an empty, spooky room
with squeaky mice inside,
It feels spiky and bare.
Emptiness lives in the heart of a
dark, gloomy attic.

***Rachel Brooks (10)***
***Hopes Hill Primary School***

## TERROR

Terror is black
It smells like dead rats in the cellar.
Terror tastes like acid burning in your mouth.
It sounds like crunching ice.
It feels sharp and jagged
Terror lives inside our soul.

***Joanna Priest (10)***
***Hopes Hill Primary School***

## JOY

Joy is orange,
It smells like Christmas,
Joy tastes like melting chocolate,
It sounds like people laughing,
It feels like new toys.
Joy lives in your heart.

***Daniel McShee (9)***
***Hopes Hill Primary School***

## MY BROTHER

My brother is sometimes sweet,
And his writing is very neat.
But sometimes he can be annoying
Because he wakes me when I'm sleeping,
And comes in when I'm playing.
He sometimes embarrasses me
And sometimes he impresses me,
But all he really is,
*Is my brother!*

***Lauren Workman (10)***
***Kingswood Primary School***

## THE ZEBRA

The grass was sweet with dew,
Munching away happily the zebra's
    mind was far away.
The zebra was in the trees,
Its family was far behind.

A hyena came to catch it
And bit the zebra's leg.
The zebra was trying to get away
But the hyena was tugging too hard.

The hyena had a tasty meal,
A meal for the flocking birds.
The last thing the zebra saw
Was the light of another day.

*Kim Terrett (10)*
*Kingswood Primary School*


## WINTER POEM

W  hen the snow is all around
I   slip and slide on the ground.
N  ow I have my gloves and hat
T  o keep me warm where I am sat.
E  very day in the soft white sky
R  eindeers fly up so high.

In the winter it is cold,
I sometimes see a lot of mould.
It is cold, there is snow,
Santa goes, 'Ho, ho, ho.'

*Tash Fry (9)*
*Kingswood Primary School*

# SPACE

Space,
Huge black and deep, as deep as the deepest hole,
Stretching for light-years around.

Solar eclipses,
The moon passes in front of the shining sun
And shatters its rays of light.
The temperature drops for a moment in time
As frightened children scream.

The Milky Way,
Each star twinkles like crystals in the sunlight,
White diamonds, blue sapphires and shimmering green emeralds
Stretching over space like a blanket,
Warming all the planets in our solar system.

Black holes
Swirling and sucking deep in space,
Kidnapping the greatest of planets,
It's strange to think that a dead star
Can do so much damage.

Space is a thing
That's been there for years
Before the human race,
It was there before the dinosaurs,
It was there to see in
*The beginning.*

***Holly Walter (11)***
***Kingswood Primary School***

## THE GAME

Long after dark
Round at the park,
Boys lurk in the rain
Waiting for the game.

To scare and to spook!
To hide and to look!

Long after dark
Round at the park,
Girls soon came
Waiting for the game.

The hooting of an owl,
The rustling of a leaf,
The engine of a motorbike
And the chattering of teeth.

Long after dark
Round at the park,
A tall boy came
Waiting for the game.

He was all dressed in black
But his face was pale white.
His T-shirt was baggy
But his trousers were quite tight.

He looked at them all
And with a sneer and a grin,
Led them in to the hedge
And what lay within.

Soon came a scream,
All but one clambered out,
Now that park's
Always empty after dark!

***Ellen Devine (10)***
***Kingswood Primary School***


## HARVEST

What's that noise?
No it's not thunder,
It's not a bulldozer.
Have a guess . . .
It is the noise of
The teeth of the tractor
Ripping up the precious corn,
And leaving the fields bare.

What's that sight?
No it's not butterflies on the trees,
It's not children climbing, having fun.
It's women climbing the trees,
Reaching for the apples
That look like gems.

When what is grown
To be picked has been picked,
And what has been grown in the ground to be pulled
Has been pulled,
The harvest is over
And silence returns to the land.

***George Williams (10)***
***Kingswood Primary School***

## HARVEST

It's harvest time,
The crispy golden leaves
Trickle through the thin breeze,
The trees are getting colder and colder
When the leaves leave the bare trees.

When the wind blows, the corn
Waves one after another
As the combine harvester nibbles
Away the corn. As the combine harvester
Rattles on, it sounds like a few windows
Hitting the stone cold concrete.

It's harvest time.

*Mark Robertson (11)*
*Kingswood Primary School*


## EVERY NIGHT

When yellow ball is shining, we come out to play,
But then later in the day
Colours form in the sky,
Reds, blues, pinks and yellows.
The colours spread in the sky,
The light catches my eye
And grown-ups call it -
    The sunset.

Then in the night it's creepy,
When you're tucked up in bed all sleepy.
You hear cars screeching round the busy bends,
You see a shadow reaching forward.
Your spine shivers as you glare,
You feel a tingle in your hair,
So this is a very big warning,
    Keep tucked up in bed till morning.

*Megan Harrison (10)*
*Kingswood Primary School*

## HARVEST

It's harvest time,
The combine harvesters are out again,
The sound of it sounds like
A million china plates dropping,
The smell of the dust lingers
In the breeze through the fields.

The taste of the wonderful fruits,
Apples, peaches and much more
And the berries like
Strawberries and blackberries,
The juices squirt into your mouth,
It's harvest time again.

*Sam Adams (10)*
*Kingswood Primary School*

## TOYS

When it's dark and you've all gone to bed
And dream of all kinds are filling your head,
Toys of all kinds are coming to life,
Dolls and figures play all through the night.

The teddies have a picnic,
They will have much fun,
Ice lollies to lick and
Lemonade and sugar buns.

The cars have a race,
On your marks get set, go.
What an excellent pace
But then some are still slow.

And then when the sun awakes again
And the day is drawing near.
The toys find their places and
Hide away their faces.

***Abigail Beswick (11)***
***Kingswood Primary School***


## WINGS

If I had wings
I would go out and touch the sun,
It would be like being burnt by a red-hot oven.

If I had wings
I would taste some fire,
It would taste as hot as a blazing fireplace.

If I had wings
I would listen to the birds fly past me like a flute.

If I had wings
I would smell the breath of the wind
Like an invisible fire.

If I had wings
I would gaze at the plants that sparkle green.

If I had wings
I would dream of going into the future or the past.

*Christie Jarrett (8)*
*Leighterton Primary School*


## WINGS

If I had wings
I would touch Venus,
Burning like molten metal,
Raging like fire.

If I had wings
I would taste a chocolate space rocket
Streaming through the galaxy.

If I had wings
I would listen to the multicoloured raindrops sing.

If I had wings
I would glare at the monstrous, large, fat
Elephants stomping.

If I had wings
I would dream of the stars
Twinkling like at the year 2001 celebrations.

*Robert Lord (8)*
*Leighterton Primary School*

## WINGS

If I had wings
I would touch the fluffy, snuggly clouds
That smell like candy.

If I had wings
I would track through the grass to see the
Tiger's soft fur coat.

If I had wings
I would smell the trees,
Swaying side to side.

If I had wings
I would glance at the stars twinkling.

If I had wings
I would listen to the people in the town,
The horses neighing, the rats squeaking,
The mice screeching, the babies wailing,
The children screaming and the birds twittering.

If I had wings
I would dream of skating in the air
With it blowing behind me.

*Harriet Wallington*
*Leighterton Primary School*


## WINGS

If I had wings
I would taste a cup of the moon in the moonlight
And watch the stars glow.

If I had wings
I would touch the delicate sun just as the moon is going down
And look at the fluffy clouds go by.

If I had wings
I would sniff the scent of the sun
And sit on the sharp mountains.

If I had wings
I would hear the birds singing
And chattering in the blue sky.

*Sarah Mould (7)*
*Leighterton Primary School*


## WINGS

If I had wings
I would touch a zombie,
Slithery and slimy.

If I had wings
I would taste the blazing hot sun like a fire,
It would taste like barbecue sauce.

If I had wings
I would listen to the stars twinkling at night.

If I had wings
I would smell the jacket potato warming up
The cold winter air.

If I had wings
I would stare at the people in the aeroplanes,
Flying all day.

If I had wings
I would dream of rivers silver,
And golden mountains.

*Joshua Tuck (8)*
*Leighterton Primary School*

## I WANT THEM CHOCOLATES

Chocolates tastes like rotten fish,
Rats on toast is my favourite dish.
Some people like decomposed flesh,
Some even like slug's guts fresh.
So give me them chocolates, come on right *now!*
Then I'll give you rotten cow.

***Callum Watson-Kemp (8)***
***Leonard Stanley CE Primary School***


## RAINBOW

R ed, orange, pink and blue,
A nd it's over the hills where the cows go moo.
I t shines in the sky,
N o reasons why.
B elow the people run from cold,
O ver the hill at the end find the gold,
W ow it's a rainbow.

***Jessica Gibson (9)***
***Leonard Stanley CE Primary School***


## A DOG AS THIN AS A RAIL

I've got a dog as thin as a rail
With fleas all over his tail.
When his tail goes flop
All the fleas at the bottom hop to the top.

***Jemma Field (9)***
***Leonard Stanley CE Primary School***

## MY BROTHER

My brother is nice and cuddly
like a teddy bear.

He is a maniac like a sumo wrestler
but as kind as a mummy horse.

When we're out he runs as wild as a tiger,
around and around the field.

When he sleeps he's like a small
red fox dreaming.

My brother is as bouncy as a kangaroo
and as silly as a clown.

He is as fast as Daddy, he is three years old
and the last thing is he is the best.

I love him and so would you!

*Amy Matthews (9)*
*Leonard Stanley CE Primary School*


## I WOULD MAKE...

I would make a computer out of jelly.
I would make a house out of chocolates.
I would make a flower out of sweets.
I would make a Zoe out of cardboard.
I would make a classroom out of gingerbread.
I would make a poster out of porridge.
I would make peace out of rainbows.

*Amelia Glassonbury (8)*
*Leonard Stanley CE Primary School*

## ALPHABET POEM

A is for apples rosy and red.
B is for blue the colour of my shoe.
C is for cat that miaows all day.
D is for the dog that barks at me.
E is for elephant that has a long trunk.
F is for fish that swim in the water.
G is for the goat that lives on the farm.
H is for happiness all around the world.
I is for igloos in the Arctic.
J is for jelly wobbling on the plate.
K is for the kettle in the kitchen.
L is for lemon that we eat.
M is for mice that squeak all night.
N is for my friend Nicole.
O is for the otter that lives in the water.
P is for the panda climbing up the tree.
Q is for the Queen that rules the country.
R is for the rat that has a long tail.
S is for the sea that flows around the world.
T is for Tarzan swinging through the trees.
U is for the unusual things that happen.
V is for Vanda that lives across the road.
W is for the windows in our houses.
X is for the extremely anxious people.
Y is for the colour yellow of the sun.
Z is for the zebra black and white striped.

*Emma Fitter (10)*
*Leonard Stanley CE Primary School*


## FLOWER POWER

Snowdrops are white,
Violets are blue,
Roses are red,
Carnations too.

Sunflowers are yellow,
Tulips are pink,
But whatever are pansies?
They're purple I think.

*Rachel Bayliss (9)*
*Leonard Stanley CE Primary School*


## I AM AN EVACUEE

On the train we went through the main part of the city.
As we got further out green started to show,
And suddenly the countryside started to show up.
I saw a cow,
My sister shouted 'Wow!
What a thing!'
And then I saw one more,
It was a chicken.
When we got off, I got my clothes and gas mask,
'Who are we going to stay with?' I asked.

*Lauren Oakes (8)*
*Leonard Stanley CE Primary School*


## ON THE TRAIN

On the train I can hear the wheels on the track,
I feel sad and on the way I see a cow,
I wonder who I'll be living with.
When we got there a lady took us to a hall,
People came to take us to a new home,
I wonder how long I have to stay.

*Kerry Prictor (8)*
*Leonard Stanley CE Primary School*

## THE DORMOUSE

    The dormouse likes to look for food,
He likes to wear a jacket,
    The big old cats like him too,
And they also want to smack it!

    The dormouse likes to sleep
In a little box,
    And he likes to steal things,
Especially your frocks.

    Sometimes they share your home,
Which I think's rather nice,
    But not when it comes to clearing up
The smelly little mice!

***Emma Stephens (10)***
***Leonard Stanley CE Primary School***


## ON THE TRAIN

When I was on the train
I felt 'clickety, clack'
On the track
And felt it go 'chug, chug'.
I felt homesick.
Suddenly the train
Went 'wibble, wobble'
And nearly fell over to the side.
Then there was a tunnel,
We had to go through it.
Then we saw some
Cows on a farm.

***Elliot Rees (8)***
***Leonard Stanley CE Primary School***

## THE TORTOISE WHO WANTED TO RUN

There once was a tortoise who wanted to run
but knew he was much too slow,
and although he was green and as small as a bean
he thought he would give it a go.

Now the animals laughed and fell about
to see such a funny sight,
of a tortoise bright green and as small as a bean
running with all of his might.

He did it again a few weeks ago
when no one was about,
and although he was green and as small as a bean
you should have heard him shout . . . *'Hooray!'*

*Alexandra Bayliss (9)*
*Leonard Stanley CE Primary School*


## ON THE TRACK

On the track, on the track,
'Clickaty clack'
On the track.
Going so fast 'Jicketty, jarsk, Jicketty, jarsk', going
Somewhere we don't know but we are not going slow.
'Triperty trap, triperty trap',
People are on the train thin or fat.
What do I feel like?
Not very right.
My brother is dull missing his mum,
You know big brothers don't get along with others.
'Clickaty clack, clickaty clack',
We've got off the train but we're not going back.

*Rory Birch (8)*
*Leonard Stanley CE Primary School*

## FOOTBALL IS THE GAME

The thrill, the fun, the game of sport,
I like to shoot, I play up front a lot.
With speed and skill I go through the players,
Passing quite often, never making any errors.
This is the sport, the one and only game,
There's nothing quite like it, there's nothing the same.
This game is all skill, there is no fluke,
There are not many mistakes and when there are they're minute.
I feel marvellous while playing this sport,
I feel disappointed it feels so short.
I think I'm quite good, second best in the school,
I think it's really fluent, the easiest sport of all.

*Timothy Williams-Ellis (9)*
*Longborough CE Primary School*


## NIGHT

I was walking down a silver road,
I saw the gleaming starry sky,
As the light reflected off the sun, it shone like gold.
Sometimes the nights are cold.
I even saw the big bright moon,
It was glistening like a gigantic ice crystal.
Now the sun goes to bed, but the shiny moon is still there.
The stars twinkle like the silver moon,
They appear one by one or maybe even in clusters.
Now the night fades away and the morning is nearly here.
Another day ahead of us,
I can't wait until night is here.

*Amy Townsend (11)*
*Longborough CE Primary School*

## RAIN

Drip, drip goes the rain,
Falling heavily on the plants and ground.
Bang, bang, banging on the rooftops,
Countless numbers of children with a severe case of boredom,
With nothing to do but boring homework,
But all you can do is wait.

Drip, drip goes the rain,
Now the rain has been falling too long,
Rushing down the garden path
Like an angry swarm of bees,
But all you can do is wait.

Drip, drip goes the rain no more,
Finally, the bang, bang, banging has stopped.
Countless numbers of children can now play outside.
The plants and ground are fresh and new,
There is no need to wait.

*Joseph Deane (10)*
*Longborough CE Primary School*


## APRIL SHOWERS

Rain, rain is a pain,
Will it ever come again?
I just can't explain why it is a pain.
Drip, drop, plip, plop,
The rain is falling.
Mum is calling,
'Quick, in you come,' she shouts.
In comes Mrs Smith short and stout,
The ducks waddle over to their shelter.

*Jessica Murray (9)*
*Longborough CE Primary School*

## THE LION

A proud elegant feline
Prowls along the safari lane,
In and out the small trees
With his swaying, spiked up mane.

On the grass nearby
Is a stubbly, scruffy zebra,
The lion stalks up on it slowly
And pounces: that I remember.

At last the lion's prey is found.
He finishes his dinner and goes to sleep by a tree.
Eventually the lion strolls back to his pack,
Like he's just eaten a McDonald's.

I sat in a jeep just watching him
As he found his own big family,
He lay down happily
As he slept on a full stomach.

My mind was twirling, twisting, turning,
Not scared but fascinated by what I was learning,
My stomach churned, burned,
The tour guide and I murmured
To each other mesmerised.

*Joe Nott (10)*
*Longborough CE Primary School*

## THE HELLMOUTH

I was standing on the edge of the Hellmouth,
Looking down I saw vampires, demons, werewolves and zombies.
God created the Hellmouth when he made the Earth.
These creatures have been attacking humanity for thousands of years.
I found out when a vampire tried to climb out to drink my blood.

The Hellmouth shook as it became dusk,
I knew this because the field it was in rumbled.
I ran away as it grew wider.
When I was far away I could still see the Mouth of Hell
Covering the field.

*Alexander Tweddell (11)*
*Longborough CE Primary School*

## THE BEAUTIFUL SEASIDE

The seaside is fun, the seaside is peaceful,
Children are playing,
Adults are shouting,
'Children, children come and get an ice cream.'
'No Mum,
Let's build a sandcastle or go in the sea.'
The glimmering, golden shore shines beneath the shimmering sun,
They dive into the blue waves and paddle in the sea.
At the beach it is warm and excellent,
They had a really good time.

*Kristie Ellery (10)*
*Longborough CE Primary School*

## DOLPHINS

Dolphins glide through the sea,
Signals passing one to one,
Through the waves and through the shipwreck
              in the peaceful sea.
Twists and turns up and down,
Dolphins live beneath the ocean grounds,
Swimming round a corner -
Never knowing what's waiting.

*Louise Griffiths (10)*
*Longborough CE Primary School*

## THE JUNGLE

The jungle is peaceful.
The crocodile is lethal.
The chunky, massive, slimy, slithering snake
                 passes by the jungle,
And the hippos are passing in a bundle.
The lions and tigers roar and scare the children away
And the children start to cry.
Elephants are stomping and it sounds like an
                 earthquake is coming.
The ostriches come and bite the adults.

*Charlotte Townsend (10)*
*Longborough CE Primary School*


## THE FIRELESS DRAGON

The dragon flew over stormy seas
To the secret isle of the Japanese.
Till at last he found the town of Hashive,
Then tucked in his wings and sped to a dive.
The dragon tried and tried to breathe fire,
But found he couldn't so turned and flew higher.
He huffed and puffed but only smoke came out,
But still the villagers continued to shout.
Eventually the dragon decided to go home,
Feeling stupid, fed up and all alone.

*Chris Burger (10)*
*Longborough CE Primary School*

## SUSPENDED IN TIME

The griffin in time is frozen.
In the wide open sea a fish-like creature is stolen,
Then a mean troll from its mountain height.
The griffin in time splits.

The griffin can fly. The fish can swim.
Can the troll fly, swim? Can he climb high?
Time stops hard.
They drift away.
They glare. They see a bridge, three Billy goats
Hopping by. 'This is my stop' said the troll.
Later the griffin flew away into his own time.
The fish to his lake does go and all is normal in time,
Except the story of the Billy Goats Gruff.

*Nathan Simpson (11)*
*Longborough CE Primary School*


## THE DAY THAT I DIVED

On a sunny, bright day
I thought I might dive,
So I jumped off a cliff
And landed in the sea.
I could not believe what I could see -
Fishes, seaweed and shells.
I could not believe that this was me.
I saw a crab and some fish hurrying by.
I don't know why
The ocean seemed a friendly place.

*Laura McPherson (11)*
*Longborough CE Primary School*

## A Spell To Create A Monster

Watch my magic, watch my spell,
Beware, the result will be hell.
Brick of wall,
Bowling ball,
Watch my magic, watch my spell,
Beware, the result will be hell.

Watch my magic, watch my spell,
Beware, the result will be hell.
Tiger's claws,
Lion roars,
Watch my magic, watch my spell,
Beware, the result will be hell.

Watch my magic, watch my spell,
Beware the result will be hell.
Bubble and bake,
Never feed him a single cornflake,
Watch my magic, watch my spell,
Beware, the result will be hell.

*Daniel Wilcox (9)*
*Longlevens Junior School*

## The Hell Spell

Bones of a boy, boiled hard,
Head of an angel, cooked in lard,
Claws of a devil that burn in the fire,
The jaws of hell to lift you higher,
Teeth of a werewolf stored in a jar,
Soul of Hitler gone too far?
Power of a trident stored in a cage,
The threat of a dragon stamping in rage.

*Mark Creese (8)*
*Longlevens Junior School*

### EARTH DESTRUCTION SPELL

Add a pinch of death,
Some blood and guts
With the head of Macbeth.
Mix the earthquake of Timbuktu,
A deadly alien,
A petrified ghost
And the explosion of you.
Add some danger,
A pinch of fire,
Sprinkle death
And a headless stranger.

***Lucy Henderson (9)***
***Longlevens Junior School***


### VIOLENT SPELL

The fist of a gorilla,
Kill it and grill it.

Teeth of a shark,
Fry them and dye them.

Claws of a tiger
Boil with foil.

Mouth of a whale,
Bake it and shake it.

A foot of an elephant,
Churn it and burn it.

***Georgina Marfell (9)***
***Longlevens Junior School***

## WORK HARD SPELL

Magic wand
Wave over my head,
Bring me alive
From my bed.

Fill me with magical
Thoughts I don't know,
Cast all my worries,
Make them go.

Add in some oil for the cogs,
And the bark of a particularly clever dog,
Make me a smart guy,
Make me less shy,
Make me work hard
So I can fly.

*Ben Kirby (8)*
*Longlevens Junior School*


## THE HELL SPELL

Bubble, bubble, badness and trouble,
Eye of lizard,
The hat of a witch,
Tongue of frog,
A scratch and itch,
Fangs of werewolf,
Eye of blizzard,
Tail of dog
Boiled and baked,
Bubble, bubble, badness and trouble.

*Laurence Mezo (8)*
*Longlevens Junior School*

## DARK POWER

Bolt of thunder,
Boil until it starts to bubble.
Smell of horse,
Make it rumble.
Dark power, strong power,
King of the bloodthirsty and dead.

Sting of killer bee,
Guts of a crocodile,
Tongue of snake,
Only mix by the Nile.
Dark power, strong power,
King of the bloodthirsty and dead.

Teeth of shark,
A pinch of rage,
Blood of a dragon,
Kept in a cage.
Dark power, strong power,
King of the bloodthirsty and dead.

Claws of a tiger,
Heart of a devil,
Scale of a sea serpent,
Now it's at the dark level.
Dark power, strong power,
King of the bloodthirsty and dead.

*Martin Feighan (9)*
*Longlevens Junior School*

## THE HAPPINESS POEM

Churn and turn
Around the fire
Till the happiness rises higher!

Laughter of vampire,
Tickle of honey
Mixed in a cauldron under a tree!

Heart of a monkey,
Huff, puff of wolf
Sprinkled in the coldness of the north!

Wool of purple sheep,
Ray of moonlight
That has fallen from a great height!

Smile of lion,
Dust from the sun
Erupts into fountains of happiness and *fun!*

Churn and turn
Around the fire
Till the happiness rises higher!

***Yasmin Kadodia (9)***
***Longlevens Junior School***

## A VERY DIFFERENT HUMAN

Bladder of Hell,
Teeth of a cat,
Tongue of a tree,
And the tail of a rat.

Left ear of Hitler,
Mad man's daughter,
The roar of a lion
Brought to the slaughter.

The black wing of a raven,
A field full of snow,
Beard of Heaven,
And the darkened horns of Diablo.

Lungs of a tank,
Fangs of Dracula,
A piece of chicken,
And all things peculiar.

***Daniel Dixon (8)***
***Longlevens Junior School***

## A SPELL TO FLY

Eye of eagle,
Blue bird's beak,
Mixed with olives on a mountain peak.

Tongue of griffin,
Leap of frog,
Carefully added in the fog.

Speed of rocket,
Boost of kite,
Only mixed whilst riding a bike.

Pinch of happiness,
Punch of light,
Only mix during the night.

Eye of eagle,
Blue bird's beak,
Mixed with olives on a mountain peak.

***Samuel English (8)***
***Longlevens Junior School***

## THE HAPPINESS SPELL

Take a pinch of love from your best friend's heart
And the bright twinkle of a star,
Taste the sweetness of a jam tart
And hear the love song played on a guitar.
Stir and fry only when it's dry.

Snatch the jewel from a bright silver bangle
And twist it until it shines in the light,
Watch it swing, sway and dangle
And glitter with all its might,
Stir and fry only when it's dry.

*Joanna Steel (9)*
*Longlevens Junior School*


## BADNESS SPELL

Wing of owl,
Tooth of shark,
Sting of bee,
Add when dark.
Pinch of crab,
Spider's leg,
Cat's claw,
Rotten eggs.
Hair from armpit,
Cuckoo's spit,
Let it brew
'Til it's true.

*Craig James (8)*
*Longlevens Junior School*

## THE CANTEEN

'Twas Friday and the sausages and chips
Did rest in greasy pools on my plate,
The ice cream melted in a yellow puddle
And the coloured plates did clatter.

'Beware the dinner ladies, my child,
The ones that shout, the ones that scream.
Beware the poisonous cooks
And shun the evil year three's.'

He took his clean knife in hand,
Long time the sausages he sought,
So rested he by a frozen pea
And sat awhile and thought.

And as in thought he sat,
The sausage with eyes of batter
Came climbing up the whirly fork
And was tasty as it was eaten.

One, two, one, two, through and through
The half-clean knife went slicing quick,
He left it greasy and with a chip,
He went chomping back.

'And have you slain the sausage?
Come to my arms my hungry friend,
Oh delicious day, *burp, burp, yum, yum.*'
He licks ketchup off his lips in joy.

'Twas Friday and the sausages and chips
Did rest in greasy pools on my plate,
The ice cream melted in a yellow puddle
And the coloured plates did clatter.

*Craig Jones (10)*
*Longlevens Junior School*

## THE PIRATE SHIP

I wish I lived on a pirate ship
jumping in the sea with a dip.

>Across the seas I would sail
>to meet the big white whale.

In my cabin I would
keep my treasure.
I would count gold
coins with lots of pleasure.

>With the Jolly Roger flying free,
>through the telescope I could
>see the sea.

My enemies walk the plank,
I would laugh until they sank.

>My cannons would be shiny and black,
>I would fire them when I attack.

My parrot is called Jumping Jack,
I don't know why I called him that.
He squawks every time he speaks,
he has a big yellow shiny beak.

>On a pirate ship I would like to be
>so I could sail across the sea.
>When I come home I'd write a book
>about that pirate, Captain Hook

*Joseph Legge (8)*
***Lydney CE Primary School***

## THE CATERPILLAR'S LEAF

        I wish I lived on a leaf, soft and green
        With the furriest caterpillar you've ever seen.
        We would live in the morning dew,
        The furry little caterpillar, just me and you.

It would be cold and wet,
The rain would come falling like a jet.
I might eat a leaf or two,
Only if you are, are you?

        Leaf to leaf I'd go,
        I'm very, very, very slow.
        I would scramble through the rainy weather,
        I'm as light as a golden feather.

I might wiggle up a tree
And do something that amazes you and me.
I will turn into a butterfly
And you will watch me flutter by.

        With caterpillar I would wiggle
        And write a book with a squiggle.
        The people would know I'm there,
        They would watch and stand and stare.

*Tessa Jones (9)*
*Lydney CE Primary School*

## THE PIRATE'S SHIP

I wish I lived on a pirate's ship
With the Jolly Roger blowing on the tip.
Where pirates go nobody knows,
From island to island off they go.

> My parrot would look so bright and jolly,
> It would squawk all day 'Who's a pretty Polly!'
> Pete the pirate was always told
> Never to pinch that lump of gold.

I fight my battles, I win my gold,
I get my bandanna which I fold.
I get my treasure that I find,
Everybody wants my gold, thieves
        queue up in a line.

> Pixie the pirate was as deep as a post,
> Pixie was scared of that ugly ghost.
> Polly was fighting, she had no luck,
> This time again she had no luck.

With the pirate's ship
I have enjoyed this sailing trip.
All the people would read my book
Just like the travellers of Captain Cook.

*Jessica King (10)*
*Lydney CE Primary School*

## THE UFO

      I live in a UFO,
           We have an alien dog called Po.
      We take him for walks around space
           While he chewed his little brown lace.

The UFO shape is a dinosaur head,
    The colour inside is a really bright red.
It's got green lights along the sides
    Which shine so brightly when we hide.

      Round the planets we go
           Riding in our UFO.
      The alien with fourteen eyes,
           On everything he does spy.

The sky is black, the stars are gold,
    On our space journey it is very cold.
The meteors crash into our UFO
    And then we go very slow.

      With the UFO I should like to roam
           And write a book when I come home.
      All the people would read my book
           Just like the travels of Captain Cook.

***Ashley Edwards, Shane Symonds & Andrew Dodds (9)***
***Lydney CE Primary School***

## THE PIRATE'S SHIP

I wish I lived on a pirate's ship,
'Lift the sails' says Captain Skip.
Where he comes from nobody knows
Or where he goes, but on he goes.

The ship has shiny black cannons,
Ten fighting sea monsters with a thousand men.
All we have to eat is a few crumbs,
Yo, ho, ho and a bottle of rum.

In the night he steals the gold,
And he is freezing cold.
All I have is a parrot
And all he has is a carrot.

The sails are white, the sea is green,
And the ship is like a battle machine!
The world is round and he can ride,
Splash and crash to the other side.

With the pirate I should like to roam
And write a book when I come home;
All the people would read my book
Just like the battles of Captain Hook.

*Niall Walker (10) & Lloyd Barker (9)*
*Lydney CE Primary School*

## THE PIRATE SHIP

I wish I lived on a pirate ship,
To eat an apple and save a pip.
I wish I had a shiny hook
So I would look like Captain Hook.

I wish I could sail a pirate ship
And have a long brown whip to skip.
I wish I could ride over scary seas
And have the secret chamber keys.

I wish I could travel with Captain Hook
And look at a very famous book.
I wish I could win a dangerous fight
And travel all the day and night.

I wish I could drink the yo, ho rum,
But there will be none left for my tum.
I wish I was the driver of the ship
And could see a great big dolphin flip.

I wish that I was Captain Hook
Then I could write a famous book.
All the children would read my book
And I will look like Captain Hook.

*Emma Fletcher (9)*
*Lydney CE Primary School*

## THE PIRATE'S SHIP

I wish I lived on a pirate ship,
I'd win a battle on every trip.
With my ship to carry me from here to there,
If I got stranded I'd send off a flare.

> I lost a leg in my first fight,
> No one is ever going to put it right.
> All we had was an annoying parrot
> And all he ate was long, orange carrots.

As we travelled over the waves
On the island we sheltered in caves.
When I travelled and fought with my sword
I always did it so I wouldn't get bored.

> The sand is yellow and the trees are green,
> I didn't get lost in them so I was always seen.
> I sailed, explored and discovered different lands,
> Then I showed the world by holding them in
>                                            my hands.

On a pirate ship I would like to roam
And write a book when I came home.
Everybody would read my book
Just like the travels of Captain Cook.

*Thomas Sollis (9)*
*Lydney CE Primary School*

## I Wish I Lived In A Lion's Jungle

I wish I lived in a lion's jungle,
To watch the monkeys swing and tumble.
I love the lion's giant hut,
To drink a drink from a coconut.

      The lions and I would roam about,
      Everyone would be loud and really shout.
      I'd get in trouble every day,
      And for food I would not have to pay.

I'd write a book when I came home
But I would still like to roam.
Everybody would know that I was here
Because my lion would roar quite near.

      I'd play about with the lion's baby,
      I'd call it Katen maybe.
      I would swim right down the waterfall,
      I would hear the lion echo when he roars a call.

I would lie about the exotic beach,
And talk to the lions in lion speech.
I would hear all sorts of different noises,
And watch the seas where I would see cruises.

*Katie Williams (9)*
*Lydney CE Primary School*

## THE HAND'S PENCIL

I wish I was a long blue pencil
So I could draw around an alphabet stencil!
Some I will do fast and some I will do slow,
When I do it fast my face starts to glow!

As I rock from side to side losing lead all the time,
Writing numbers and words, some that rhyme!
As the sharpener sharpens me
They use me as a door key!

As they put me in the pencil pot,
It's very cold but kind of hot!
They bite me, they suck me, they call me a he,
I'm not really a he, I'm a she!

I get shorter and shorter, smaller and smaller,
But everyone knows that you can't get taller!
As it twirls around I get dizzy,
My hair is all straight and fizzy!

When I wiggle into the pencil pot
I'd write a book about how to jot.
I'd wiggle around on the paper
And wait till it is much later.

*Tiannie Bowery (8) & Danielle Watkins (9)*
*Lydney CE Primary School*

## THE SEAL'S PUP

I wish to live in the sea,
With the seal pup I would be.
In and out the caves he goes
To smell the fishes with his nose.

Rainbow fishes swimming round,
Glistening and swimming without a sound.
Golden coral waving in the sea,
Loads of fishes one, two, three.

Swimming swiftly through the coral reefs,
Going over, right, left and underneath.
Swimming with the fishes golden brown,
Swimming, zooming, looking down.

With the seal pup I wish to swim
And never want to leave him.
I'd write a book when I come back
And empty outa water-filled sack.

*Gabrielle Olley (8)*
*Lydney CE Primary School*


## GREEN IS . . .

Fresh of summer
rising above us.
Adventure here we come.
We feel the morning
breeze while the whispering
of leaves in the jungle
come towards us.

*Samantha Cairns, Rebecca Young & Holly Tarrant*
*North Cerney CE Primary School*

## GREEN IS...

Green is the colour of the grim, gungy slime
dripping from the stalagmites in the cave.
Grass glowing in the light of the moon.
Trees flashing before your eyes making them
glow as bright as a diamond.
Moss spread along a wall like cement.
Mould all over a London house window.
Sleep in the gaps of your eyes.
The shoot of a plant just beginning its life.
Seaweed on a sandy beach.
A Hindu temple roof gleaming at you.
A sea monster's footprint glowing with green.
A palm leaf shading the tourists.
The colour of a fire exit showing the way.
The colour of a raincoat out in the storm.
The colour of a caterpillar moving about the ground.
A green gem floating in a pirate chest.

*Joseph Johnson (10)*
*North Cerney CE Primary School*


## PURPLE IS...

The colour of allied jealousy,
A part of autumn plants,
A poisonous horn,
Thick liquid,
A berry in the summer,
The bag of the eye,
The beast's blood,
The sunset sky.

*Linden Moy, Sam Greenwood & Christopher Horton*
*North Cerney CE Primary School*

## FIRE

Fire is like popcorn
crackling
in the pan.

                    Like a dragon's
                    gleaming
                    scale.

Like a lion's mane
beaming
in the sun.

                    Like snakes
                    flickering
                    over leaves.

Like a lion
roaring in
the background.

***Isabella Horton (11)***
***North Cerney CE Primary School***


## YELLOW IS...

Bright sunshine on
a spring day,
A polished necklace,
A thirsty holidaymaker
on a beach,
Fresh clean and crisp air,
A tall sunflower reaching
for the light.

***Thomas Franklin & Jack Hale***
***North Cerney CE Primary School***

## GOLD IS ...

Gold is a desert that spreads with sand,
And stars gleaming in the night sky
That sparkle as bright as a light,
The royal king happy with his crown,
Car lights flashing bright, the light might blind you,
It smells like money, gold is money, it's treasure,
Also it looks like the summer sun
That shines on us and makes us hot,
And dead grass in the wind, then the grass changes colour,
The cut wood looks yellowish in the middle
And yet looks like gold,
Coins rustling like someone smashing glass,
The sun shining on the deep blue sea.

*Luke Ellis (10)*
*North Cerney CE Primary School*


## MY IMAGE OF THE SEA IS LIKE ...

My image of the sea is like
a flexible cushion, as flexible as can be,
a tossing saddle taming the creatures below,
a whale crying out for love,
the sea is sinking for the boats lie,
the boats sway, the waves clash,
but the sea is quiet now, it is no more
for humankind killed it!

*Lianne Katie Weeks (9)*
*North Cerney CE Primary School*

## CHOCOLATE BROWN IS...

A muddy, impure, wet outside day,
A shivering woodland smell that comes out of nowhere,
A walk down a dilapidated path through a dead forest
In the middle of winter,
A freshly planted vegetable patch in autumn,
A confectionery store with children buying their
Weekly stock of sweets,
Lifeless stormy days where the rain is pitter-pattering on the roof,
A dim, careless child who has been playing in the mud
And got herself mucky,
A bitter cold chomping away at your fingers,
A filthy, grimy, gritty pile of compost just waiting to be turned,
Mud-splattered rain rolling on saturated stones like melted
Chocolate on a sponge cake.

*James Tarrant (11)*
*North Cerney CE Primary School*


## BLUE IS...

The sound of wind
rushing at you,
Boats drifting away,
A deep enraging anger
trapped inside you,
A moon controlling
a crashing ocean.

*William Seymour, Joe Walker & Nicholas Holder*
*North Cerney CE Primary School*

## FIRE

Fire is like a spirit
floating
in a combusting redness.

Like a planet
flaming
its gas.

A horse
galloping
at you.

The carpet
of God's home.

Blood
boiling in your head.

Like the Devil's kingdom.

The rainbow's colour burning.

The smoke of a dead bull.

A witch's spell
glowing
with anger.

A holy spirit
gleaming
with pride.

*Joe Johnson*
*North Cerney CE Primary School*

## MR GREEN

Mr Green is
informal and untidy.
He carelessly treks
across the forest
floor dragging his
ripped trousers
over the ground,
his bobbly jumper
swaying in the wind.
His spindly fingers
wrapped round his
walking stick.
The soles of his shoes
are as flat as pancakes.

*Ben Barton, William Seymour & Robert Gardiner*
*North Cerney CE Primary School*


## THERE ONCE WAS A TOY CALLED PING

There once was a toy called Ping
Who couldn't stop trying to sing.
He sang to a mouse
Who lived in a house
And ended his life as a king.

*Victoria Turner (9)*
*Northleach CE Primary School*

## A TREE

The morning dew gleams on my emerald leaves.
I see tiny birds sweetly singing as they build
Their nests in my many branches.
A light breeze ruffles my sweet blossom.
I feel children tickling me as they climb my long body,
A twig snaps,
I sway with excruciating pain.
I see a man coming towards me carrying a long toothed object,
The machine starts to spin,
It saws through my precious branches.
They drop to the ground like dead birds,
The man leaves without a sound.

*Ayla Kelly (10)*
*Northleach CE Primary School*


## I WAS SO THOUGHTFUL

I was so thoughtful that I heard
the clouds drift
lazily across the turquoise sky.

I was so pensive that I heard
the caterpillars arguing over
who would be the prettiest butterfly.

I was so reflective that I heard
the dictionaries competing for
which one has the most complex words.

I was so meditative that I heard
the distant murmur
of leaves as they turned their golden colours.

*Charlotte Fothergill (11)*
*Northleach CE Primary School*

## A POEM TO BE SPOKEN SILENTLY

It was so silent that I heard
balloons itching to be blown up.

It was so silent that I heard
an instrument clatter in its box.

It was so silent that I heard
a leaf fall off a tree.

It was so silent that I heard
the walls moaning to be covered.

It was so silent that I heard
a pencil scratching to write.

It was so silent that I heard
my clothes rattling in the wardrobe.

It was so silent that I heard
my computer mouse rolling on its mouse mat.

*James Clayton (11)*
*Northleach CE Primary School*


## TEDDY BEAR

I am sitting on the bed waiting,
So lonely, so dull.
Here she is,
So here I go!
Oh no I'm squashed,
Help! Help!
Ahhh I'm not squashed now.
Here I go to watch TV
On a nice comfy sofa.

*Alexandra Goddard (10)*
*Northleach CE Primary School*

## A Poem To Be Spoken Silently

It was so quiet I could hear the sun
shining in the east.

It was so peaceful I could hear the teddy
saying, 'Hold me and cuddle me.'

It was so still I could hear the itching
powder itch and crackle.

It was so soft I could hear the map
thinking which way to go.

It was so calm I could feel the blood
running through my body.

It was so still I could hear the dictionary
spelling out all the words.

It was so motionless I heard Jack Frost
crackle as he laid his snow.

It was so frozen I could hear the pencil
scratching itself on the paper.

It was so peaceful I could hear the bed
creak 'Goodnight.'

*Sarah-Louise Morgan (10)*
*Northleach CE Primary School*


## My Cat

Bird eater
Tree climber
Leg scratcher
Sleepy snoozer.

*Jasmine Burns (9)*
*Northleach CE Primary School*

## THE EPITAPH GRAVEYARD

Here lies the body
of a very mad wizard
who was frozen one day
by a passing blizzard.

Here lies the bones
of a deadly lizard.
He was zapped one day
when he attacked a wizard.

Here lies the bones
of Cherie Blair.
She died one day
from her husband's stare.

Here lies the body
of a poor old goat.
He drowned one day
when he tried to float.

*Joe Sellwood (11)*
*Northleach CE Primary School*


## CHARLES

Voice overuser
Mouth widener
Tongue bouncer
Max amuser
Glad gobber
Good friend.

*Samantha Norman (10)*
*Northleach CE Primary School*

## THREE EPITAPHS

Here lies the bones
Of a great big lizard,
Who died in the middle
Of a mighty blizzard.

>Here lies the body
>Of a great giant frog,
>Who tried to eat a
>Very big dog.

Here lies the bones
Of Charles Meacher,
Who got on the wrong
Side of his scary teacher.

***Charles Meacher (10)***
***Northleach CE Primary School***


## THE OAK TREE

I feel lonely and hurt being bashed and hit by the wind,
Being beaten and thrashed by the rain,
Cut and stabbed by the hail,
But feel warm and loving to the sun
That helps me grow to a grandfather oak.
The sun will keep me warm, repair my wounds
And make me feel loved.
Helpful, I may be helpful to you and to a bird,
But how do you repay me?
By cutting me down.

***Amy Edwards (11)***
***Northleach CE Primary School***

## WINTER

I rise from my summer's sleep to the winter's mist,
I fly through the misty winter's air scattering my frosty flakes
                                    into the icy land,
Icicles appear on the gutters of houses,
They crash on to the icy floor.
I lay my white cloak on the ground and see children playing on it.
I see the ponds freezing,
I say 'What a fabulous sight.'
Suddenly I swoop down to the ground and throw snow into
                                    children's faces.

*Bradley Spedding (11)*
*Northleach CE Primary School*




## TREE

I hear the birds making a nest,
Sometimes I really think they're a pest,
Twittering, twittering.
My leaves will grow now,
I am really happy and thrilled,
But how do my leaves grow?
My leaves blow until I'm tired,
Here it comes, my leaves are beautiful.
The flowers are tickling my roots,
It is like a pair of boots on my roots,
The spring colours are lovely.

*Imogen McConnon (10)*
*Northleach CE Primary School*

## SILENT

It was so silent that I heard the books
barging each other to get more space.
It was so peaceful that I heard the water
vibrate in my bottle.
It was so relaxing that I heard the book
rattling its pages.
It was so quiet that I heard the pencil
itching to write.
It was so still that I heard the light bulb
saying, 'I'm too hot.'
It was so calm that I heard a singing
voice coming from the town centre.
It was so silent that I heard something
strange coming from a toy.
It was so restful that I heard the tissues
rocking in the box.
It was so untroubled that I heard birds'
eggs hatching in their nests.

*Simon Page (9)*
*Northleach CE Primary School*


## WINTER

I start to wake and paint the leaves different colours.
I set my frosty concrete on the branches of the trees.
Suddenly I feel a rush of excitement and I rush down
The road taking out fences as I go.
Now I hear a strange noise, the sound of sparrows singing,
It seems my time here is now done, so back to sleep I go.

*Max Yates (10)*
*Northleach CE Primary School*

## MY BROTHER

Kick-boxer
Food snatcher
PlayStation master
Brain buster
Cool dude.

*Amy Hubbard (9)*
*Northleach CE Primary School*

## MY PIG

Hand sniffer
Food guzzler
Sty sleeper
Mud lover
Heavy trotter.

*Joanna Rainey (10)*
*Northleach CE Primary School*

## RAIN

It's raining, it's pouring
It's so dreadfully boring
My bike's in the shed
There's tears on my bed
What can I do?
Not much it's raining.

*Natasha Didcote (8)*
*St David's Primary School, Moreton-in-Marsh*

# CARS

Cars can go very fast indeed
They can go at top speed
Push the accelerator to make it go
Hard for fast and soft for slow.

Cars can come in many colours
Which one would be yours?
Blue and white
Would be alright
Red or green
Are easily seen.

Racing cars are very fast
Go too slow and you'll be last
If you come upon a curve
You will not want to swerve.

Racing cars are the best
If you lose that is a pest
A cup will go to the best
Nothing will go to the rest.

A car needs lots of petrol
And a lot of oil
The tyres go round
And make a screeching sound.

Windscreen wipers go up and down
If they didn't you would frown
Windows go up and down too
And let fresh air in when they do.

Cars can go to different places
Stops us having to go a few paces
Please don't take my car away
Or I can't go on holiday.

*Daniel Abrahams (9)*
***St David's Primary School, Moreton-in-Marsh***

## THE NOISE FROM NOWHERE

I heard a scratching somewhere,
    It stopped, all I could hear now was footsteps.
I wondered if there would be more,
    The scratching was quiet, there was a small noise.

I heard a noise like a miaowing sound,
    I thought something was hurt.
There was a sound like something was going round,
    I wondered what it was.

I looked around, nothing was there,
    I heard the sound again,
I looked down the hall,
    Nothing was there.

I looked in the kitchen,
    Nothing was there.
I looked in the bathroom,
    Nothing was there.

The scratching noise
    Was getting louder,
I didn't dare go through
    The passageway.

*Becky Udell (9)*
***St David's Primary School, Moreton-in-Marsh***

## SUMMER FLOWERS

In my gaze I sit and stare
At all the flowers pink and fair,
I watch the flowers sway to and fro
As the gentle winds blow,
They last a whole season, what more could you ask?
They bloom up bright in the tall, long grass,
Scents of perfume nectar attract the bees
From their honey-filled trees,
In the brook I sit and play
Watching the flowers brighten the day,
The trees provide shade,
The sun provides heat,
The rain provides moisture for the flowers to eat,
Patterned petals provide beauty and colour for all,
Walking the meadows I stumble and fall,
Summer flowers are pretty, cheerful and light,
They make everyone happy, joyful and bright.

*Emma Norton (10)*
*St David's Primary School, Moreton-in-Marsh*


## BEAR

He is very, very round,
He's big and brown,
He's very, very chubby,
And has got a big, hairy tummy,
He loves to eat honey,
Yum, yum, yum!
And to give me a hug to say he is happy,
He sits in the corner all alone,
Waiting for someone to take him home.

*Alice Byrne (10)*
*St David's Primary School, Moreton-in-Marsh*

## SPACE

Space is a big place,
with the Milky Way and planets,
and meteorites, zooming around in space!
Space is a gigantic place,
light years and light years apace,
we're all in the race,
going round the sun!
Pluto is the coldest of our planets
like a skiing run!
The opposite of the sun.
There are many stars in space,
but only one we've seen,
that's the sun in this huge place.
A flying ball of gases!

*Samuel Evans (10)*
*St David's Primary School, Moreton-in-Marsh*


## SNOW

Walking down the fields,
In the crispy snow,
Crunch, crunch, crunch, it's horrible.
I wish I was home, it's freezing,
Crunch, crunch, crunch.
I am only two fields away,
It's as white as a sheep and as cold as a fridge,
Crunch, crunch, crunch.
There's all that foamy snow, it's horrible.
I'm just one door away from home
It's all sticky,
Now I'm home I'm happy.

*Sam Turner (9)*
*St David's Primary School, Moreton-in-Marsh*

## SPACE

The USA have been to the moon,
They'll probably want to go back there soon,
All the aliens look like goblins,
Houston we have a problem!

Plant Earth is green and blue,
All forms of life live on it too,
The ozone is all around it,
Pollution could destroy it!

The sun is boiling hot,
It has big, red burning spots,
If you get too close,
You would be a Sunday roast!

The universe goes on forever,
Let's hope it will all stay together!

*Katie Foylan (10)*
*St David's Primary School, Moreton-in-Marsh*

## ROUND, BROWN CONKER

Round, brown conker,
as snug as a bug in the ground,
a little leaf for its quilt,
going to sleep ready for next year,
to grow in the spring.

*Esme Baggott (8)*
*St David's Primary School, Moreton-in-Marsh*

## BOOKS

Books, books, wonderful books
All different shapes and sizes
There are even some with surprises.

Some are fat, some are small,
Even very rare and very tall.
Books, books, please take a look,
Because you might learn how to cook!

Some are happy, some are sad,
If you don't read them, you will go mad!

I like to read,
So take my lead,
I love books,
Books, books, wonderful books.

*Leigh-Anne Woskett (10)*
*St David's Primary School, Moreton-in-Marsh*


## LIGHT

The candle is light
Twinkling at night
Sparkling so bright
Some are big
Some are small
You buy them at the shops
Where you buy lollipops
So light one tonight.

*Kate Burrows (8)*
*St David's Primary School, Moreton-in-Marsh*

## THE BEACH

The beach is made of golden sand,
the sea is aqua-blue,
children playing hand in hand,
having loads of fun too.

The sun is shining brightly,
the black clouds have gone away,
people crammed together tightly,
together children play.

In the distance boats sail out to sea,
people paddling up to their waist,
splashing as if they were free,
running through the waves as if being chased.

Eating out of paper, their fish and chips,
a boy playing with his bucket and spade,
looking in the water at faraway ships,
and patting a sandcastle he has just made.

*David Groom (11)*
*St David's Primary School, Moreton-in-Marsh*


## THE SEA

It's like a wild wolf tearing the rocks from the cliffs,
and yet it can be like a baby or a cat asleep
but it can be like a bull seeing red
it can be like a stream running gently
it holds life in death
it holds danger
it holds mysteries.

*Leo Newman (11)*
*St David's Primary School, Moreton-in-Marsh*

## END OF SCHOOL

Dring goes the bell for the end of school
boom, bang, crash through the doors,
nudge, jostle, trying to get your bag and coat.
Stomp, stomp, stomp you go zooming down the stairs,
screech, turn a corner and bash through the doors.

Running across the playground, up over the gate,
zipping up the road overtaking cars,
whizzing through the gate of your house.
Smashing through the door,
leaping on the settee ready for watching tele,
now you're nice and relaxed.

*Jake Wright (11)*
*St David's Primary School, Moreton-in-Marsh*




## SHADOWS ON THE SEA

When the day is hot,
The beach is full.
The sea is pleased,
Whirling, dancing, hopping and jumping
The shadows begin to play.
Whirling, dancing, hopping and jumping
The sea laughs and waves her waves.
The end of the day, the beach is empty,
But the sea is still pleased.
For the sun has not yet had his fun
The sea is still pleased.

*Daisy Perry (9)*
*St David's Primary School, Moreton-in-Marsh*

## THE WEAKEST LINK

The Weakest Link's on TV
I watch it every night,
I really like Anne Robinson,
She puts up such a fight.

The people on the show,
Try hard to get it right,
For if you get it wrong Anne,
Says goodnight.

The questions are so hard,
And Anne Robinson so tight,
Contestants are so stressed,
They want to get it right.

The way to finish my poem is like on the show
You are the weakest link - so go.

*Niall Arthurs (11)*
*St David's Primary School, Moreton-in-Marsh*

## HOMEWORK

Boring, boring homework
We have it every day
The more we do, the more boring it is
We prefer to run and play.

Boring, boring homework
We always hate it so
It is packed with maths and science
So it's really hard to do.

Boring, boring homework
It really is a bore
So quickly go and hide it
And hope nobody saw.

*James Henshaw (11)*
*St David's Primary School, Moreton-in-Marsh*

## RAIN

One day it started to rain,
Drip, drop, drip, drop, drip,
Then it rained even harder,
Splishy, sploshy, drop, drip,
But . . . it rained harder,
*Splash! Splash! Splash! Splash!*

Then it started to thunder,
Boom! Boom! Boom!
But it woke up the baby,
Waah! Waah! Waah!
You could hear the cars go
Beep! Beep! Beep!

The thunder stopped
And the rain calmed down,
Pitter-patter, splosh, splish.

The baby stopped crying,
Dad started snoring,
Honk! Shhh! Honk! Shhh!
And do you know what Mum whispered
She whispered this,
Shhhhhhhhhh! Shhhhhhhhh!

*Jodie Harrison (9)*
*St David's Primary School, Moreton-in-Marsh*

## SPACE

Outer space is a big, big place,
There must be more than the human race
Could there be beings apart from mankind?
What is there out there, what could we find?

Planets and stars, Pluto and Mars,
Little green men riding in cars
Spaceships and shuttles will help us to find
If others are out there, who also have minds.

The sun is the centre of our galaxy
It gives off the heat that allows us to be
Could there be other suns out in the dark
Triggering life's mysterious spark?

*Thomas Barton (10)*
*St David's Primary School, Moreton-in-Marsh*


## VALENTINE

You are my valentine again,
You rock my world inside my brain.
You have a great sense of humour,
But wish you could have used it sooner.
You are the best ever seen
A foxy, poxy teenage teen.
I guess it's time to say farewell,
Now you've gone, I'll cry and yell.

*Chelsea Dyer (10)*
*St David's Primary School, Moreton-in-Marsh*

## CANDLE

A little candle small and round
sitting on the dark, damp ground.
Its flickering flame up all night,
and in the morning light and bright.
It's done its best, now it's put to rest!

*Alexandra Parker (8)*
*St David's Primary School, Moreton-in-Marsh*

## GREEN

G reen is the fields and leaves on a tree,
R ibbiting frogs in a pond,
E xotic fruits in a greengrocer's shop,
E merald gems, deep green in colour,
N ew buds in spring.

*Jennifer Rolton (10)*
*St David's Primary School, Moreton-in-Marsh*

## CRICKET RESOLVE

I'm a pace bowler takin' every wicket,
That's what I want to do
We should beat the Aussies this year
but if we beat Sri Lanka
I will cheer a cheer.
Pace bowler and in the slips -
that's what I'll achieve next year!

*Sam Reeves (9)*
*St John's Primary School, Cheltenham*

## THIS YEAR

This year will be the year
When I get everything right.
This year will be the year
When I learn to write.

This year will be the year
When I learn to draw.
This year will be the year
When I learn a lot more.

This year will be the year
When I learn to spell.
This year will be the year
When school turns out well.

This year will be the year
When I learn to run.
This year will be the year
When work turns to fun.

This year will be the year
When all my problems are solved.
This year will be the year!

*Charlotte Cambray (9)*
*St John's Primary School, Cheltenham*


## MY CAT

I would love to get along with my cat
She hates me, she really does
The only time she likes me
Is when I give her treats or food.

My cat can get very evil
Especially when you tease her
She starts to spit and hiss
But if you treat her nicely
She'll loudly start to purr.

*Carrie Knight (9)*
*St John's Primary School, Cheltenham*

## MY BROTHER IS AN EARTHLING

My brother is an Earthling
I'd like to be just like him,
He eats brown things called chocolates
And chucks paper in the *bin*.

We go to school in things called cars
The ugly, green contraptions,
The noisy teacher shouts, 'What's this?
Sit up and pay attention!'

He plays things called computer games
He really is quite good,
But after a while he always cracks up
I always would know when he would.

But that's enough, I really can't think
You suppose I'm an alien,
I am a human like anyone else
I'm just one normal schoolboy, age 10.

*Sam Thacker (10)*
*St John's Primary School, Cheltenham*

## Resolution

I want to improve
my behaviour at school
I know I'm getting better.
It used to seem impossible
to have a lesson without jabbering on
I used to daydream about eating a scone.
So come on Laurie,
You've gotta improve
Cos you know that it's not impossible -
to make that move!

*Laurie Wright (9)*
*St John's Primary School, Cheltenham*


## Tidying My Room

Tidying my room,
It's a great, big mess,
A tidal wave of toys

All the toys are mine
I know I have to do it,
I always put it off!

I wish I could fly and go away
and leave my pigsty far behind.
Only this year it won't be a mess,
because this is my *resolution!*

*Micky Gibbard (8)*
*St John's Primary School, Cheltenham*

## ANOTHER YEAR

One year later,
another year older.
It's time I put my head together
and learnt a little more.

There's maths I could do better,
because there's always something wrong.
There's English I could improve,
because it's never quite right.
Then there's science I need to work at,
because there's so much more to know.

One year later,
another year older.
I hope I get my head together
and achieve a little bit more!

*Leah Evans (10)*
*St John's Primary School, Cheltenham*


## RUBBISH!

Rubbish should go in bins,
unless you are naughty.
Bin it, put it in the bin.
Bin it, put it in the bin.
I will if I have to!
Shall I? Yes! OK!
Help the environment,
put it in the bin!

*James Martin (8)*
*St John's Primary School, Cheltenham*

## THE MAGIC SCHOOL BUS

The magic school bus drifted slowly,
Up above the stars so lonely.
Where there was nowhere to play,
Up above the stars today.

Suddenly, there was a bang,
And the school bus turned and ran.
Across the whole, entire world,
Up around the stars he whirled.

All across the raging seas,
Watching birds, as you please.
Then he suddenly saw a bay,
With people walking along astray.

Carefully watching with his eyes,
Seeing the faces full of surprise.
As he flew along the path,
He had a little laugh.

Suddenly, he saw his star,
And decided he had gone too far.
Swooped and twirled all the way,
That is all, for today.

*Peter Williams (10)*
*St Lawrence Primary School, Lechlade*


## BEACH RIDING

I was travelling on a horse
through the soft sand.
As we ran the sand flicked up.

I see the heavy pebbles
as they lay still in the water,
the waves splash over them.

I felt happy and excited
as I rode back across
the sand.

I get off my horse
and put him away,
until I come back another day.

*Stacey Carter (11)*
*St Lawrence Primary School, Lechlade*


## MY MAGIC MAT

Me and my mat are best of friends
When it comes to our adventures
They are scary, sad or relaxing.

When we visit all sorts of different people
Like people who don't have anything
Or people who have lots of things.

We go high and we go low
Over things and under things
Look out the bridge. Duck!

As we fly up to the sky I get excited
I wonder where I'm going today
And why are we here?

Yesterday I travelled over the city,
Through the smoke, dirt and grime.
Cough, cough, cough, watch out for the wall
I managed to splutter my way home.

Today I'm travelling along a blue, pretty, clean river
Also there is a school by this river
Say hello to the kids.

*Emma Cashin (10)*
*St Lawrence Primary School, Lechlade*

## MY PETS

I'm on my pet spider and I know he's very hairy,
with eight legs he looks even more scary.
I don't mind if he crawls up the wall.
I don't mind whether he's big or small.
I like my spider, he makes me laugh,
As long as he does not share my bath.
He's magic I tell you, he's flying in the sky,
when we come back from our journey
we will have apple pie.
I have a pet goldfish called Dotty
on her tail she's a bit spotty.
She swims up and down,
and acts like a clown.
She leaps for joy,
when I introduce Roy.
My fishes only need a feed
but my friends' pets need a lead.
She now has a friend
and all the time they drive me round the bend.
When I clean their tank out
they always begin to shout.

*Laura Jones (10)*
*St Lawrence Primary School, Lechlade*


## TRAVELLING

Travelling on a dog
brown, stripy and kind.

Travelling in the countryside
with green leaves like a green slide.

Travelling in the city
with big, tall buildings and lots of noise.

Travelling in the desert
sand in my face.

Travelling on the sea,
the water by my feet.

Travelling with my dog
just him and me.

*Jamie Tanner (11)*
*St Lawrence Primary School, Lechlade*

## HORSE RIDING

I was travelling on a horse
He was gentle and soft.
His coat, a lovely ginger
With a white diamond on his forehead.

Travelling in the countryside I saw
Trees and hills and a little stream.
I saw a sheep on the horizon
I saw a tourist walking down the hill.

I saw a man walking his collie
He threw the collie a ball.
He raced after it
The man and the collie walked and played with the ball
I saw them walk back home.

I feel happy as I gallop up the hill and gallop down again
Oh no! I hurt my hand
Never mind, I'm back on again and going as fast as ever
At last I reach my final destination
We are on the hill as we watch the sun go down.

*Vicky Challoner (10)*
*St Lawrence Primary School, Lechlade*

## MY INVISIBLE DOG

My invisible dog is not much fun
I don't know whether he's sad or glum.
When I want to pat his head
I end up patting his behind instead.
When I take him to the vet
I have to tie him down with nets.
When we get there he grabs,
And instead of him I get the jab!
My dad you see doesn't approve,
He's into cats with hip, hop, groove.
And one that he cannot see,
Just sends him up the tree.
We never are bothered with leaving doo on the street,
As you know it's invisible too.
We put up a sign that read, 'Dog for sale',
And when my dog saw it he let out a wail!

*Megan Kennedy (11)*
*St Lawrence Primary School, Lechlade*


## TRAVELLING

In the sky
I'm on a helicopter
Big, black and shiny
The city below.

In the sea
I'm on a boat
Long and thin
I can see fish.

On the ground
I am on a bus
Big, black and high
I can see the buildings rush by.

*Geoffrey Harding (10)*
*St Lawrence Primary School, Lechlade*

## PRIT STICK CHRISTMAS

My mum used Prit Stick, instead of lipstick
and went to kiss my dad.
Two days past, they both stuck fast
the biggest snog they ever had.

They pulled and pulled and were about to unstick
but Mum got frustrated and gave out a kick.
My dad gave a yell and then gave a shout
but as they were stuck they couldn't fall out.

Santa came down with a 'Ho, ho, ho,'
then looked in his bag and said 'Oh no.
Well I've got a sander and I've got a drill
I know what I'll use, an unsticking pill.'

With lips jammed tight and hardly any room to breathe,
Santa said, 'I'm late on my rounds' and had to leave.

With Santa gone and no help, none at all
Then from the tree came a little call.
The fairy witch came from the Christmas tree said
'Do not be afraid and do not worry,
my magic wand, my little stick will help your parents
both unstick.'

And they did.

*James Somers (11)*
*St Lawrence Primary School, Lechlade*

## BOAT TRAVEL

Travelling in a boat
red, green and white.
Travelling on the river,
like a graceful swan.

I can see the lock-keeper's cottage,
decorated with attractive flowers.
Pink, red and violet
all spread out in lovely patterns.

I feel happy as can be as I carry on,
and as if I have never been happy before.
Quick, move, there's another boat coming,
now I feel scared, very, very scared.

Finally I reach my destination
with a soft bed of grass.
Beautiful scenery for miles and miles,
I can't wait till I travel back.

*Rachel Leonard (10)*
*St Lawrence Primary School, Lechlade*


## THE MAGIC TAXI

The magic taxi flew quickly,
over the buildings really loudly,
flying over all the cars,
dodging all of the big, silver bars.

Taking passengers here and there,
dropping them off, some here, some there,
some passengers fat and thin,
and other passengers small and slim.

The taxi driver was feeling sad,
because he ate something really bad,
then he crashed into a pile of bricks,
and his car broke up into little bits.

He saw a man with a belt,
and asked him for some help,
they fixed the car but the metal was bent,
then the front had a big, black dent.

*Kien Lieu (11)*
*St Lawrence Primary School, Lechlade*


## THE DARK

The dark is all around you,
persuading the moon's pale face to glow whiter than snow.
The dark is all around you,
encasing your soul in a dimension of night.
The wind lashes out at you
like a terrifying horseman cracking his whip at the dark sky.
The frost bites your ears
as its pointed fingers scratch your icy-cold cheeks.
The cool dew forms under the soles of your shoes
drowning the dark green grass.
The dark is all around you,
weighing you down and substituting air.
The dark is all around you,
closing in on you, choking you, *killing you.*

*Christopher Carroll (10)*
*St Lawrence Primary School, Lechlade*

## SPACE

Rainbow planets and shooting stars;
Planets with names like Earth or Mars;
Silver ships, that fly so high;
Past secret worlds, where aliens lie;
Comets darting, to and fro;
A spaceship crashes, oh no!
Brilliant lights, that sparkle and shine;
Alien burglars, hey, that's mine!
Rocky craters, so big and wide;
Moon buggies there, for people to ride;
This trip to space, has been great;
I'll go again, it's a date!

*Joshua Nicoll (11)*
*St Lawrence Primary School, Lechlade*


## SPACE

How about going some place new,
Up in the space, just me and you.
On a voyage in the galaxy,
With aliens called Spalloxies.
In a spaceship, up we fly,
Like a kite so very high.
Up, up, up, here we fly,
Up, up, up, in the sky.
So here we are on the moon
We have got here, not a moment too soon.

*Piers Powers (11)*
*St Lawrence Primary School, Lechlade*

## FRIENDS IN FLIGHT

As I drift through the sky
cascading gently as I fly.
My wings spread out nice and wide
turning quickly from side to side.

I then turn left and then turn right
my house is just about in sight.
I wave goodbye to the forest and stream
and all alone, soar on in my dream.

Drawing closer - to a tree,
I see a bird just like me.
I circle round, then land right there
the leaves are shed, the branch all bare.

We wanted to see the world together
we'd find our adventure whatever the weather!
We preened our feathers ready to go
the mountains in the distance were covered in snow.

Over the peaks, rugged and raw
the icy mist which made our eyes sore.
We glided back to a much warmer vale
we fed by the river then upwards did sail.

Summer returned and the trees are in flower
our wings felt heavy with each passing hour.
My house began to appear close once again
and we landed nearby in a shower of rain.

*Kieran Gandhi (11)*
*St Lawrence Primary School, Lechlade*

## MY PET CAT

I have a pet cat,
She has very soft fur
And when I stroke her,
At me she will purr.

I have a pet cat,
She's very strong and tame,
And when I called her from her bed,
Back to me she came.

I have a pet cat,
Once she found a rat,
He was by the wall,
That was by the mat.

I have a pet cat,
Once a noise she heard,
Then she looked up in the sky,
But it was only a bird.

I have a pet cat,
In her blanket I made her wrap,
Then I put her in her bed,
And she had a catnap.

*Morwenna Bennett (8)*
*St Paul's CE Primary School, Gloucester*


## A DRAGON

Dragons going out of their caves,
'Here we go!'
Flying over sand dunes,
Turning them to glass,
Breaking into mirrors,
Journeying so far.

But here comes the dragon,
Ra, ra, ra.
Burning all the houses,
Fluffing up the smoke,
Running down the subway
Help, help, help!

*Edward Hood (8)*
*St Paul's CE Primary School, Gloucester*

## IT'S HOT!

It's hot in ancient Egypt,
And the land just seems to grow.
It's hotter than you think,
And for you to ever know.

It's hot in ancient Egypt,
And the land just seems to grow.
It's a great place for a holiday,
You get to wear cool clothes!

It's hot in ancient Egypt,
And a very long way too.
There's lots of things to see,
And there's lots of things to do.

It's hot in ancient Egypt,
And there's lots of things to see,
There's lots of things to play,
And there's lots of things to be.

It's hot in ancient Egypt,
And the food just seems to grow,
There's lot for you to do,
And lots for you to know.

*Candice Williams (9)*
*St Paul's CE Primary School, Gloucester*

## LADY MACBETH

L ady Macbeth is half to blame for death
A nd whilst trying to live a lie the guards are on the high
D aggers are used for this bad crime
Y ou will be king said three strange witches.

M urder of the king now done
A nd Macbeth is getting scared
C an they take the pressure off getting caught
B ut will Macbeth give in?
E vil witches set this up
T o do such an evil deed they should die
H eath they met to be told he would be king.

*Sam Azmayesh (11)*
*St Paul's CE Primary School, Gloucester*


## CHILDREN ARE ANIMALS

C ool Callum the cat is crunching cat food
A my alley cat is chilling out
T om the tiger tags tamely
S ally snail likes eating salad.

A ndy adder slithers slippery
N ancy newt is nude!
D angerous Daffy Duck's dancing.

D onn the donkey is eating doughnuts
O liver octopus is eating Amy's oysters
G eorge the giraffe is a gangster
S ammy squirrel screaming sadly.

*Michael Witts (9)*
*St Paul's CE Primary School, Gloucester*

## LADY MACBETH

L ady Macbeth married to Macbeth
A king was murdered
D uncan was killed in his sleep
'Y ou will be Thane of Cawdor,' said the three witches

M acbeth, guilty of murder
'A dders fork and blind worms sting'
C ourageous Macbeth
B anquo also co-leader of the Scottish army
E nters Macbeth, with bloodstained daggers
T his story is good because of the killing
'H eath!' that's where the witches lived.

*Ryan Faherty (10)*
*St Paul's CE Primary School, Gloucester*


## LADY MACBETH

L ady Macbeth smears blood over the guards
A nd Macbeth has hands stained with blood
D uncan is killed by Macbeth
Y elling for help was Macbeth

M alcolm was son of Duncan
A nnoying daggers floating about
C astle where Duncan died
B attle with Banquo against the English army
E vil witches tell stories to Macbeth
T remors all over the wood
H eath where the witches meet.

*Stephen Hood (11)*
*St Paul's CE Primary School, Gloucester*

## DINOSAUR BEHAVIOUR

'Dinosaur, dinosaur' just hear that *roar!*
Dinosaur, dinosaur, not crawling at all.
Scare you all to death it would,
If you ever saw,
This big, this real live *dinosaur!*

Teeth like icicles, smell of meat,
He would eat a whole fishing fleet.
Don't mess around with this mean dinosaur.
He'll eat you up right there,
He is no use to anyone,
He'll just give you a *big scare!*

King of the dinosaurs,
Shredder of trees,
He's a t-rex and . . .
'Look out, he's coming!'

*Christina Read (8)*
*St Paul's CE Primary School, Gloucester*


## MACBETH

M  acbeth, guilty of murder
A  ngry people discover death
C  old-hearted Macbeth feels sorry for himself
B  lood all over the guards
E  scape from the murder
T  ired of waiting to see who killed the king
H  ours have gone by but still don't know.

*Joe Young (11)*
*St Paul's CE Primary School, Gloucester*

## LADY MACBETH

L ady Macbeth has no fear
A ggressive she is
D on't worry are her words
Y our hands are stained with guilty blood
   is what she tells Macbeth.

M urderer she is
A venge is what she likes
C an't you face doing the deed, is what she says to Macbeth
B ewitched she is with evil deeds
E nough she has done to go to Hell
T omorrow she will dread
H ow is she to be found out?

*Rachel Bown (11)*
*St Paul's CE Primary School, Gloucester*


## DRAGONS

Dragons are nice,
Dragons are sad,
Dragons can be moody.

Big dragons are smelly and horrible,
Dragons are fierce and mad,
Dragons smell like smoke,
Flames come out of their mouth.

Dragons are scary,
Dragons are bad,
Dragons have smooth backs,
Dragon wings are very nice.

*Tamara Birch (7)*
*St Paul's CE Primary School, Gloucester*

## THE GIANT TRAIN

One day a giant train came from nowhere,
When it moved it went bang, bang, bang!
It was yellow, red and green,
It was bigger than ten thousand houses,
It went bang, bang, bang!

Me and my friend were in town,
We climbed on the roof,
We jumped down,
It was going very, very fast.
We were on the train,
Standing on chairs,
The people looked like dots,
And the cars looked like ants.

*Jamie Douglas (7)*
*St Paul's CE Primary School, Gloucester*


## MOUSETRAP

Cat said, 'Mouse, mouse, come out of your house,'
'Only if you give me some cheese.'
'Say please.'
'Please.'
'No!'
Then the cat said 'Get out here now!'
Then the cat had an idea.
Cat was thinking.
The owner of the cat is back.
He's bought a mousetrap.
Mouse comes out . . .
*Snap!*
Poor mouse!

*Ryan Barnard (8)*
*St Paul's CE Primary School, Gloucester*

## SWEETS

Sweets are yummy for our tummy,
Some are big,
Some are small,
And some are gummy.

I like sweets because some are hard
Some are soft,
Some melt,
And some don't.

My mum says, 'Don't eat sweets before your tea!'
'I like sweets too!' says my friend.
'Do you?' I say.
She says, 'Yes!'
And we all shout
'We love sweets!'

***Hannah Blackwell (9)***
***St Paul's CE Primary School, Gloucester***


## I WISH I WAS A ...

I wish I was a lion,
All cute and cuddly,
Roaring 'I am the king of the jungle!'

I wish I was a parrot,
Flying over mountains,
Squawking!

I wish I was an octopus,
Swimming through the sea,
'Where did that crab go?'

***Jack Parry (7)***
***St Paul's CE Primary School, Gloucester***

## A Shadow

Shadows, shadows are scary
Shadows, shadows are nasty
Shadows, shadows are ugly
Shadows, shadows are horrible
Shadows, shadows are stupid
Shadows, shadows are silly
Shadows, shadows go to sleep
Shadows, shadows read books
Shadows, shadows draw pictures
Shadows, shadows eat sweets
Shadows, shadows go to the shop
Shadows, shadows play in the garden
Shadows, shadows dance
Shadows, shadows play in the water
Shadows, shadows play in the sand
Shadows, shadows snore.

*Jade Barnes (7)*
*St Paul's CE Primary School, Gloucester*


## Shadows

I see shadows,
I shiver and shake,
When I wake up,
I go under my pillow,
I see the biggest shadows,
They look like . . .
Mum is coming to get me,
What shall I do?

*Jamie Allen (9)*
*St Paul's CE Primary School, Gloucester*

## MY GRANNY'S ROCKING HORSE

My granny's rocking horse
Is carved and brown like oak
It is cool to play on
And to hang your coat.

She had it when she was four
It stood the test of time
But when my granny died
She said that it was mine.

My granny's rocking horse
As old as old can be
I will give it to my children now
Now I'm thirty-three.

*Hannah Price (10)*
*Slimbridge Primary School*


## MY BOXING GLOVES

My boxing gloves are made of gold,
And my brother can fight the pros.
The pros will win and my brother will lose,

He gave a good fight,
And if he had won, he would be top
But now he is bottom because he lost
With a knock.

*Ricky Hewer (11)*
*Slimbridge Primary School*

## THE PAST

In the past we've had,
The Romans,
The Anglo-Saxons,
The Greeks,
The Victorians,
And funnily enough
*You!*
The time you were born,
The time you took your first step,
The time you said your first word,
The time you started to read this poem,
The time you started to read this line,
The time you started to read this *word*.
The past can be two million years ago,
The past can be two seconds ago,
Now can you see the past?

***Harriet Osborne (10)***
***Slimbridge Primary School***


## MY BROTHER

My brother's had his hair cut,
As short as short can be.
He thinks that he looks really cool,
As cool as cool can be.

My brother's had his hair cut,
As shaved as shaved can be.
He thinks that he looks really ace,
As ace as ace can be.

My brother's had his hair cut,
As bald as bald can be.
He thinks that he looks really fab,
*But I do not agree!*

***Abigail Poulton (10)
Slimbridge Primary School***

## SHOPPING

When I go shopping
It's so much fun,
Especially when the
Sales are on.

We buy lots of clothes
And go to Burger King,
I like it in the shops
When S Club 7 sing!

I like New Look
I like Clair's,
I like Tammy
Who sell flares.

Here come the music shops,
HMV,
Hits 2000,
Is the music for me!

Bye!

***Hannah Brown (10)
Slimbridge Primary School***

## THE WILDLIFE TRUST

Down at Slimbridge,
To see them is a must.
Are the beautiful birds,
Of the wildfowl trust.

Geese are honking,
Swans are gliding through the air with ease.
Ducks are loudly quacking,
While people feed them, hoping to please.

Peter Scott was the founder,
Not for him a tragic journey.
Where would you rather go,
Here, or South Cerney?

***James Whetherly (10)***
***Slimbridge Primary School***


## SCHOOL

I don't really like school,
But I quite like PE,
I hate all the teachers,
And the teachers don't like me.

When it is wet play time,
Most kids watch TV,
But some turn on the radio,
And listen to Slim Shady.

When we go out at play time,
I usually play football.
Some climb on the climbing frame,
And only a few of them fall.

And then it's time for us to leave,
We gather up our notes,
We're so delighted it's 3 o'clock,
We rush and grab our coats.

*Andrew Foster (9)*
*Slimbridge Primary School*

## POOR OLD GLENIS

'Please Miss, Glenis is wedged in the door,'
Six weary children tug laboriously in awe.
'No, don't do that Doris, you're such a fool,'
Here comes the door frame, fixings and all!
But alas! Down comes the wall.
Thirty-six children rush into the hall.
'Quick class, into the playground!'
Class IIB having transformed to a mound.
Ah, here comes the head, all in a fluster,
'Hurry, I need all the strength that you can muster!'
Ten bedraggled children scramble from the floor,
'Oh dear, Glenis is stuck in the door.'

*Simeon Koole (10)*
*Slimbridge Primary School*

## Autumn

Crisp brown leaves,
falling from the trees.
Red ripe leaves,
floating in the breeze.

Girls playing
with boys outside.
Stuck in the mud,
in the freezing cold breeze.

Leaves are floating
in the puddles cold.
Freezing like the sea,
always like the knee.

Leaves are golden brown,
they make me want to frown.
I wish spring would come
to turn it around.

Winter comes first,
with snow on the ground when there are no leaves around.
Then here comes spring with blooming trees with all their new leaves.

*Sophie Tremlin (9)*
*Slimbridge Primary School*


## The Shaggy Dog

The shaggy dog gazes out into the murky distance,
Its dark brown hair hangs over its wide-open eyes,
One ear tilted and another one pricked and alert.
His head slightly tipped to one side,
His everlasting, waggy tail, stopped now between his legs.

His wet nose smells the bracing fresh air,
His fur is long and tangled,
A soft brown it could be,
He is whimpering gently, scared and afraid,
He turns his back from the sight,
The shaggy dog runs away from the sea.

*Hannah Koole (10)*
*Slimbridge Primary School*

## DOWN AT THE GLOOMY WOOD

Down at the gloomy wood near Berkeley Castle
There are dark misshapen shadows that will surely frighten you.
The trees are unusual, all shapes imaginable,
The fruits are poisonous, and a funny colour.

There are also monsters in this frightening wood
With big googly eyes and crooked noses.
Their snouts are long and snorty,
Their hair's like springy spaghetti.

There are pixies and gnomes running about this wood.
No humans have ever seen them, as they are very timid.
Their eyes are like dark black buttons,
And their noses like crooked twigs.

These pixies and gnomes are surely real
As they leave all bits behind when they run.
Human contact is never made,
So none of the animals know anyone's around.

*Natasha Frewer (10)*
*Slimbridge Primary School*

## THE HAUNTED HOUSE

The house on the hill,
Abandoned and cold,
Has everyone scared
Hearing tales from the old.

Tales told about people,
Disappearing, never returning
Finding blood on the pathway,
Finding fires, still burning.

One day, a young lad,
Duncan by name,
Heard about this house
And thought it rather a game!

He wore a pan on his head,
Welly boots on his feet,
He marched up the great hill,
Ever so steep.

'Oh look,' he exclaimed,
For a sign on the door,
Read 'Home Sweet Home',
Never seen that before!

He knocked on the door,
Feeling ever so brave,
'Twas opened by a lady
Looking ever so grave.

That was enough for him!
He was scared out of his wits!
He thought he was brave,
Yeah, right! What a twit.

*Ceri Wills (11)*
*Slimbridge Primary School*

## THE FOOTBALL MATCH

22 boys,
All playing football,
At Wednesday break,
At primary school.

Knock down three teachers,
And twelve little kids.
Not even noticing
When they knock out Miss Lidds.

Take out four more teachers,
And the rest of the class
Soon the whole school
As they play on the grass.

Now of the whole school
Only Headmaster is left
Comes to put a stop to this
Chaotic event.

He goes down too,
Along with the rest.
Only the boys left,
Playing their best.

*Helen Hanstock (11)*
*Slimbridge Primary School*

## A Panda's Lifestyle

The panda lives in the forests of Asia.
It uses leaves to make a home
And you never see them come out of their home alone.

Its fur is black and white,
And it has a jet-black nose,
And sits up in the trees and shows off with a pose.

The panda will eat most vegetation including
Leaves from trees, which they will eat
With the greatest of ease.

The panda is nearly extinct.
These animals are very rare
And it feels like nobody really cares.

*Katie Frewer (10)*
*Slimbridge Primary School*


## Poems Are Great

Poems are great, I rate them high
I'll read them forever until I die.

I write them at school, all the time
Sometimes I even make them rhyme.

I sit with my mates, we write them together
We always enjoy them whatever the weather.

They're better than comics, they're better than fiction
They are my real, real addiction!

*Robert Cullimore & Owain McFarlane (10)*
*Swindon Village Primary School*

## My . . .

My brother is a pain
I don't even pull his hair
He gets me into loads of trouble
But I don't really care.

My little black guinea pig Tom
Is *so* cute!
He likes to play with his brother
But he likes to play with me too.

My dad is a massive nutter
He's even madder than me
I know this is *bad*
But it isn't even true.

My room is a tip
It looks like a bomb's hit it
They don't like it but they have to put up with it
'Cause I am just like that.

My handwriting practice is simple to do
Just think of a poem to write
And hopefully you'll get your pen licence
Like I did but not for this.

My teacher is Mrs Mills
I am in her class
But I wish I was in the other
'Cause the other is a joker.

My poem doesn't scan
Explained my dad
'I know that,' I replied
But I do so like to fit in as many words as I possibly, possibly can.

*Charlotte Brewer (10)*
*Swindon Village Primary School*

## ON THAT GREAT BUT AWFUL DAY

Floating like a cork on the sea,
There was only just time for a quick farewell.

On that great but awful day.

The chug of the engine echoed around,
The birds stopped flying, the steamer was alone.

On that great but awful day.

There was the rock,
Just like a knife from the stone.

On that great but awful day.

How it happened no one knew,
It was over just like that.

On that great but awful day.

Down went the sun,
Up went the flares.

On that great but awful day.

Down it went just like a stone,
The people bobbed around but that was the end.

On that great but awful day.

People cried on that great but awful day.

*Simon Langley (11)*
*Swindon Village Primary School*

## RAINY DAY

The rain was thundering down on the ground,
The puddles were big
The ground was as slippery as ice
And it was too wet to dig.

The children wanted to go outside
But the teacher said 'No.'
All the children moaned,
They just wanted to go.

*Peter Griffiths (7)*
*Swindon Village Primary School*

## SNOW

The snow was falling in the middle of winter
The children were playing in the soft snow.
The snow was as white as a sheet of paper
The snow started to melt and I had to go.

*Dhru Mistry (7)*
*Swindon Village Primary School*

## THE FLOWING RIVER

Gushing over, ever over
Rocks and boulders, pebbles, stones.
Down and down the river carries,
On and on for evermore.

*Shona Wilson (10)*
*Swindon Village Primary School*

## IT

An It comes from outer space,
Looking for luscious trees and roots.
It ripped roots from rocky ground,
Eating roots it rotted its ragged teeth,
No one can describe how disgusting It was.

*Matthew Evans (9)*
*Swindon Village Primary School*

## My Kitten

The newborn kitten lies still and calm,
She even fits upon your palm,
She doesn't stir, she doesn't move,
Her fur is so silky and so smooth.

She is four weeks old and now can see,
The world around her, even me,
She still stays very close to Mum
Who washes her all over with her rough tongue.

She's one year old now and fully grown,
Someday she may have kittens of her own
For now she's happy to spend each day
Lounging in the sunshine ready to play.

*Debbie Lloyd (10)*
*Swindon Village Primary School*


## The Magic Box

Into the box, with great delight,
I will put a starry night,
A wailing storm,
A ginger cat,
The magic of a flying bat.

The cute panda eating more bamboo,
The things best friends will always do,
A silent, sleeping koala bear,
A comb running through my golden hair.
I shut the lid and seal it tight,
Then leave it till the dead of night.

*Charlotte Morris (9)*
*Swindon Village Primary School*

## THE FOUR SEASONS

Spring is windy
Spring is getting hot
Sometimes you get rain
Which is why we plant flowers in the flower pot.

Summer is scorching
Summer is when we get shade
Summer is when we go to the beach
Especially with our bucket and spade.

Autumn is when the leaves fall off the trees
You could get a gale
The cats get fleas
When I have a gale my face turns pale.

Winter is cold
Sometimes it snows
Winter is when we go sledging
Sometimes the rain overflows.

*Kelsey Lonergan (7)*
*Swindon Village Primary School*


## THE THUNDERSTORM

The thunder was growling
Rain was hammering down on the pond
The wind was howling
Snapping could be heard
The branches were coming off their hinges
Trees were covering over the grass.

*Tamara Morgan (8)*
*Swindon Village Primary School*

## HALLOWE'EN

This is Hallowe'en, this is *Hallowe'en!*

I am the monster hiding under your bed,
very sharp claws and eyes glowing red.
I am the monster lying under your stairs,
snakes for fingers and a spider in my hair!

This is Hallowe'en, this is *Hallowe'en!*

I am the vampire hanging down your chimney,
you'd better watch out or I'll bite you on the neck.
I am the cyclops crying in your cupboard
with one big eye, looking through the wall!

This is Hallowe'en, this is *Hallowe'en!*

*Steven Wootten (10)*
*Swindon Village Primary School*


## MY WEATHER POEM

I like the summer
With hot sunny days
All the cold days
Start to cast away.

In the winter
It's really cold
And the trees are bare and bald.

In the autumn
It gets colder
And the trees are
Getting balder.

*Nathan Roberts (7)*
*Swindon Village Primary School*

## My Winter Poem

It was a cold and windy day.
I play snowball fights
And I can go sledging down the hill.

I like autumn because
I can play conkers with my friends
And I can jump in the leaves
And I like to ride my bike.

In the springtime
The flowers start to grow
The new lambs are born
And the grass we can mow.

*Jack Stanley (8)*
*Swindon Village Primary School*


## The Summer

The summer is hot
It's good for swimming
That's why a lot
Of the Egyptians wear linen.

In the summer
I like to tease
And run away
From the bees.

In the summer
I pretend to climb a tower
But really it's a tree
And I try to see which is the prettiest flower.

*Milli Cornock (8)*
*Swindon Village Primary School*

## THE FOUR SEASONS

Summer is my favourite time of year,
The sun shines and the days are warm,
We have loads of water fights in the backyard,
And the air smells of flowers and freshly-cut lawns.

In the winter the weather is cold,
I get excited when it begins to snow,
Children dress up warm in hats and gloves,
And make snowballs which they love to throw.

In spring lambs are born and play in the fields,
Birds sit in the trees and sing,
In the garden flowers start to grow,
I love the spring.

In autumn leaves on the trees turn brown,
They fall to the ground, circling around,
In the fields the farmer harvests his crops,
And sends them to shop keepers to sell in their shops.

*Matthew Adair (7)*
*Swindon Village Primary School*


## THE FOUR SEASONS

Spring is quite warm
It is quite windy
Spring is when we play inside
We always play with Sindy.

Summer is when you see the sun
It is really hot
Summer is when we always have fun
So we get to play a lot.

Autumn is when the leaves fall off
You could get a gale
Sometimes autumn is misty
Which makes my skin go pale.

Winter is very cold
Particularly when it snows
Winter is when you go sledging
Sometimes the rain overflows.

*Molly Chapman (8)*
*Swindon Village Primary School*


## THE FOUR SEASONS

In the spring it is warm
In the spring it is mild
The rabbits all hibernate
And the foxes go wild.

In the summer it is hot
You can go swimming
And lie on beds
And start sunbathing.

In the autumn it is getting colder
And the conkers start to fall
You can no longer play
Or do summer volleyball.

In the winter it is cold
You can have snowball fights
The winter gets the snow
You can have snowboard flights.

*Adam Knowles (7)*
*Swindon Village Primary School*

## AUTUMN

Autumn leaves come off the trees
And fall to the ground
They fall gold and brown
Then they roll around.

The sky is grey and black
Sometimes there is brightness
And sometimes there isn't
But the sun give us lightness.

Rustle by
Crackle and crunch
Hustle by
In a snippety bunch.

*Janine Irwin (7)*
*Swindon Village Primary School*


## SUMMER

Summer is lovely
At summertime it's very hot
Everyone is happy
In this season flowers are growing in a pot.

Summer is nice and warm
It's very cool
I go sunbathing on the beach
And I go to play in the pool.

The flowers are coming out
The sun is shining bright
Bees are flying all around us
We have a wonderful night.

*Tanya Hopson (7)*
*Swindon Village Primary School*

## DIFFERENT MONTHS OF THE YEAR

I like to play in summer
I like it best when it's hot
We go to many places
So I get to play a lot.

I hate it when it's cold
And windy and rainy and wet
It's not fun at all
I would rather be at home with my pet.

I do like summer
But the best is when it snows
I like to play in snow fights
And best of all I like to make snowmen
With a big red nose.

*Louise Rogers*
*Swindon Village Primary School*




## THE BOBCAT

Bobcat waits till dark for its prey
Now it's dark, it's time to hunt
Starts walking slowly
And carefully to the long grass
He walks into it and looks around
He sees something rattling
It comes closer
The bobcat sees it, out comes a snake
The bobcat carries on.

*Thomas Warnes (8)*
*The Moat Junior School*

## IF YOU WANT TO SEE A TIGER

If you want to see a tiger
You must go to the smelly jungle
I know a tiger who's living down there -
He's mean, he's big, he's fierce
Yes, if you really want to see a tiger
You must go down to the smelly jungle
Go down and say
'Stripy, stripy'
And from the grass, a tiger will come
But don't stay there
*Run for your life.*

***Zak Hayes (8)***
***The Moat Junior School***


## THE WEATHER

What is thunder?
Somebody stamping
Why does it rain?
Somebody's crying
What are hailstones?
Big balls falling
Where does wind go?
In one ear and out the other
What is fog?
White fluffy clouds
What is snow?
White cotton wool
What is the sun?
Big ball of fire.

***Kelsey Goodwin (11)***
***The Moat Junior School***

## IF YOU WANT TO SEE A BEAR

If you want to see a bear
You must go to the dark
And spooky woods

I know a bear who's living there
He's mean, he's scary and
Very, very fierce

Go quietly down to that wood
And say
Daddy bear
Daddy bear
Daddy beaaar!

And he'll rise with a shriek
But don't say for long
Run for your live!

*Danielle Thornhill (8)*
*The Moat Junior School*


## IF YOU WANT TO SEE A TIGER

If you want to see a tiger
You must go down
To the green, dark forest.

I know a tiger who's living down there
He's mean, nasty, cheeky and growling.

Yes, if you really want to see a tiger
You must go down to the green, dark forest
Go down to the forest and say 'Tiger, dada tiger
Dada tiger, dada tiger, dada.'

*Mark Sysum (8)*
*The Moat Junior School*

## IF YOU WANT TO SEE A TIGER

If you want to see a tiger
you must go to the very
end of Spain

I know a tiger
who's living down there -
He's wicked, he's big, he's fierce
and he's man-eating tiger

Yes, if you really want to see a tiger
you must go to the very end of Spain

Go down to the very end and say
tiger, tiger, tiger, tiger, tiger, tiger
tiiiiger.

And he will come out
but run away or he will get you.

*Nina Foot (7)*
*The Moat Junior School*


## WEATHER

What is a rainbow?
A coloured bridge falling over the sky
What is snow?
Birds' feathers from the sky
What is the sun?
A big football shining in the sky
Where does the snow come from?
From Santa's chimney
Where is weather from?
Another galaxy.

*Ross Farrell (11)*
*The Moat Junior School*

## WEATHER

What is thunder?
Angry lions roaring
Where does the sun come from?
A super, hot galaxy
What is a rainbow?
A coloured bridge
Where does snow begin?
At Christmas time
What is a tornado?
A giant mad house sucker
Where does wind come from?
The angels blowing
What is hail?
A giant ice cube
What is a earthquake?
Angels stamping their feet.

*Kieron Fitzgibbon (11)*
*The Moat Junior School*


## ANIMAL POEM

Mice scuttle,
Dogs bark,
Cats strut,
Elephants trumpet,
Lambs frisk,
Pigs grunt,
Leopards roar,
Chickens squawk,
Penguins waddle,
But -
I talk.

*Rosanne Dowding (9)*
*The Moat Junior School*

## QUESTION AND ANSWER POEM

Where does the snow begin?
When the snowman fills with joy.

Why does it rain?
It rains because God's jolly.

Where does the wind blow?
In the north where the funny penguins go.

What is lightning?
Disco lights, where the angels dance.

Why does it get foggy?
It makes it easy for the green Martians to land.

What is frost?
Jack Frost's friends in the cold.

Why does a storm start?
Miss Cloud is fighting with her husband.

*Kelly Miles (10)*
*The Moat Junior School*


## WEATHER

What is thunder?
It is lions roaring in the sky.
What is a rainbow?
It is crayons drawing in the air.
What is lightning?
It is birds with torches flashing.
What is the wind?
It is clouds blowing a breeze.

*Shaun Huntley (11)*
*The Moat Junior School*

## WEATHER

What is a rainbow?
A colourful arch leading angels to Heaven.

When does snow begin?
When fluffy white clouds begin to burst.

How does snow begin?
It tumbles off Santa's sleigh.

When do you hear thunder?
When a big, black cloud begins to burst.

How does fog appear?
When a big, grey cloud is shot to the ground.

Why does the sun glow?
Martians are shooting flame throwers at it.

What is weather?
Nobody knows.

***Christopher Partlett (10)***
***The Moat Junior School***


## THE WIND

I can blow people over,
And lift them off their feet,
Go through a doorway
Without a key,
I'm happy just being me!
Being the wind is so much fun,
I blow umbrellas inside out
And battle with the sun.

***Samantha Turner (9)***
***The Moat Junior School***

## WEATHER

What is a rainbow?
A brightly coloured bridge falling over the sky.
How does thunder come?
A man bellowing out his rage.
What is rain?
A gigantic sprinkler on the Earth.
Where does the wind begin?
When the expanding turbines pick up speed.
What is the sun?
A golden football thunderously kicking into space.
Where does ice come from?
A freezer left open.
What is fog?
A smoke machine at a disco.

*Daniel Wright (11)*
*The Moat Junior School*


## WEATHER

Where does snow begin?
When white fluffy clouds begin to rot.
What is a rainbow?
A colourful archway leading dead people to Heaven.
Where does mist come from?
It's when a cloud trips over his own legs.
What is a hurricane?
A golden eagle flapping his gigantic wings.
Where does the sun come from?
A person throwing a huge light bulb into the dark sky.

*Samuel Critchley (11)*
*The Moat Junior School*

## WHAT IS WEATHER?

What is thunder?
Two angry lions roaring ferociously.

Why does it rain?
Because somebody left the tap on.

What are hailstones?
Sparkling diamonds, glistening on the icy ground.

Where does the wind go?
In one ear and out of the other.

What is fog?
God's fluffy electric blanket being laid down on the Earth.

Where does snow come from?
Someone's having an enjoyable pillow fight.

What is lightning?
A blaze of yellow developing in the ochre sky.

Why does the sun shine?
To make people smile!

*Zoe Carter (11)*
*The Moat Junior School*


## NURSE JILL

Nurse, come quick
Teddy's been sick
Dolly is looking quite pale
And Piggy is in bed with a very sore head
And Tiger has hurt his tail.

*Charlotte Owen (9)*
*The Moat Junior School*

## WEATHER

Where does the sun come from?
From a super, hot galaxy.

What is the sun?
A yellow, soaring sword.

Why does the wind blow?
Because the fluffy clouds are puffing.

How do you catch the wind?
With a gulp of your mouth.

Why does it rain?
Because God lets his bath water out.

What is snow?
Snow is buds off little cotton wool.

Where does the sun go at night?
Under the blue ocean.

*Emma Willetts (11)*
*The Moat Junior School*


## THE WIND

I'm the wind, don't you know.
I have the best blow
I'll blow your knee if you try me
Soon you'll learn to like me
If you think you're better than me
Find me and I'll blow some wind on your body.

*Tyrell Williams (9)*
*The Moat Junior School*

## WEATHER

Where is snow from?
From Santa's chimney.

What is the sun?
A present from God.

Where is weather from?
A million light years away.

What is snow?
Clouds that are sprinkled at Christmas time.

What are hailstones?
Hard balls of snow.

What is rain?
Little drops of water that fall from the heavens.

What is a rainbow?
Colours that cover the Earth like a bridge.

*Lee Gordon (10)*
*The Moat Junior School*


## THE WIND

I blow people's roofs off,
Get under their doors,
Without any key.
I take people's hats off
And think that's funny.
I snatch wheel trims
And tear off soft tops.
I'm really naughty.

*Josh Rogers (9)*
*The Moat Junior School*

## THE WEATHER

What is a rainbow?
A colourful archway leading the angels to Heaven.

When does snow begin?
When big, white, fluffy clouds begin to burst.

How does snow begin?
It tumbles off Santa's magic sleigh.

When does it thunder?
When a big, black angry cloud explodes.

How does fog appear?
When a big, cloud gets shot to the ground.

Why does the sun glow?
Martians are shooting flame throwers at it.

What is weather?
Nobody knows.

*Stephen Fitt (11)*
*The Moat Junior School*


## WEATHER

W  indy day nice to play,
E  very day I like to play,
A  nd I go to play today,
T  ime to wrap up nice to stay,
H  eat today nice to stay,
E  very day it's nice to play,
R  ain to stay not so good.

*Stacey Lee (9)*
*The Moat Junior School*

## SNAKES

Fangs shoot poison -
Giving nasty bites,
Watchful, evil, beady eyes, flickering
With no warning pounces,
Waving its vicious forked tongue.
Hissing noise as it spits poison,
Unpleasant to touch
Scary patterns,
Quickly slithering towards you -
With no warning!
Beware of its blind spot,
If you don't want a surprise.
If it eats anything -
It might just be you.

*Class 3B*
*The Moat Junior School*


## CHOCOLATE CHIPS

Chocolate chips
Coloured dips
Nasty nips
Fingertips
Licky lips
Chocolate whips
So many things to choose
I just can't lose
But the thing I like the best
That certainly tastes better
Than the rest, is my . . .
*Chocolate chips.*

*Elisha Blackwood (11)*
*The Moat Junior School*

## THE WEATHER

What is a rainbow?
A colourful archway leading the
angels to Heaven.

When does snow begin?
When big, white, fluffy clouds
begin to burst.

Why does snow begin?
It tumbles off Santa's magic sleigh.

When does it thunder?
When a big, black angry cloud explodes.

How does fog appear?
When a big cloud got shot
to the ground.

Why does the sun glow?
Martians are shooting flame-throwers
towards it.

What is weather?
Nobody knows.

*David Black (10)*
*The Moat Junior School*


## WATER

W et and soapy
A nd all bubbly,
T he most common substance in the world,
E asily found in the tap and the ground,
R ecently found in caves.

*Steven Partlett (8)*
*The Moat Junior School*

## BABYSITTER

Pitter-patter, nitter, witter
Where is the babysitter?

'Babysitter come on in,'
Little Neil has hurt his shin.

She reads him a story and tucks him to bed,
Little Neil, sleepy head.

Babysitter goes downstairs to watch TV,
While little Neil has dreams of glee.

Mummy and Daddy come early from their night out,
Daddy's foot is hurting, he's got gout.

Here's five pound,
Was Neil sound?

*Holli Thompson (9)*
*The Moat Junior School*


## WEATHER

Where does white snow begin?
When white fluffy clouds start to break.
How does the wind blow all of the snow back?
It blows it back to the clouds strongly.
Where does the hail come from?
When they're dropping silver bombs down from Heaven.
Where does thunder come from?
When fierce lions start to fight.
When do brightly coloured rainbows come up?
When people start to draw.

*David Clarke (10)*
*The Moat Junior School*

## WEATHER

What is a rainbow?
A colourful brick bridge leading up to the sky.
What is lightning?
A huge electric fault in God's beautiful Heaven.
What is fog?
A grey sheet of cloth protecting the sky.
What is snow?
When God's and angels have a fun pillow fight up in Heaven.
Where does the storm begin?
When people are bad and God doesn't like it.
What is thunder?
When God's tummy rumbles.
What is wind?
A huge breezy breath of air.
What is the sun made up of?
Boiling hot particles binding up together.
What is weather?
A lot of God's minds performing together.

*Vicky Scott (10)*
*The Moat Junior School*


## FOOTBALL

F ierce football I don't like,
O h! When it is raining it is boring,
O h! It is hot, let's play,
T he good thing about football is when you score,
B all bounces in the air,
A man scores
L oads of cheering,
L a, la, la.

*Josh Hawkins (8)*
*The Moat Junior School*

## THE WIND

I can be a gentle summer's breeze -
When I'm happy, I'm really okay,
But if I'm angry, I'll blow you away!
I howl and blow with all my might,
I'm invisible as a ghost, haunting at night.
As my force gets stronger,
I destroy streets and blow down trees,
I blow lamp posts over,
I blow ships and make them sink,
I take old men's walking sticks
And blow people over -
Lifting them off their feet -
I blow people off their bikes,
Blow hats and coats away -
I have the best blow!
I sing with the rain,
I splash in puddles
And battle with the sun.
When I blow a gale,
I howl like a ghost.

*Class 3A*
*The Moat Junior School*

## THE WIND

I'm the wind,
I can blow hats and cats,
I'm the wind,
I can blow frogs and dogs,
I'm the wind,
I can blow leaves
And big oak trees.

*Ashley Caine (8)*
*The Moat Junior School*

## ANIMALS AND ME

Mice squeak,
Dogs bark,
Pigs grunt,
Lions roar,
Cats spit,
Hamsters bite,
Goats chew,
Horses gallop,
Birds whistle,
Lions stalk,
Mice creep,
Deers leap,
Rabbits jump,
Caterpillars hump,
Puppies bounce,
Kittens pounce,
Seagulls glide,
Snakes slide,
*But I walk,*
*I talk!*

**Danielle Dillon (9)**
**The Moat Junior School**

## THE WIND

I blow people over,
Knock people's hats off,
I make people freeze,
I go into houses every day -
Sometimes I even knock the roof off a house!
I lift humans off the ground because I'm strong,
I'm really sad because I've got no friends.

**Sam Myatt (8)**
**The Moat Junior School**

## I'VE LOST MY CAR

I've lost my car, I've lost my car
It's nowhere to be seen
I've lost my car, I've lost my car
And it was red and green

I've found your car, I've found your car
Outside the baker's shop
I've found your car, I've found your car
I am a clever cop

A clever cop, don't make me laugh
You've no brains in your head
The car I lost was red and green
That one is green and red.

*Giorgette Bendle (8)*
*The Moat Junior School*


## THE WIND

I can blow over trees because I'm really strong
I'm like a tornado but not that big
If I'm angry
I'll blow you away
If I'm happy
I'm really okay!
I can blow dogs and cats
Blow off your hats
I'll blow your hair
I'm really unfair!

*Jade Stevens (8)*
*The Moat Junior School*

## ALIENS

Once I was visited by aliens!
They took me across the galaxy!
We saw Saturn with its gleaming rings,
Icy and cold as we flew past.

Next we saw Mars, the red planet,
Aliens' colonies running around
Jupiter next the gassy planet
Reds and greens flashed by
Mercury closest to the sun
Hotter than the Sahara Desert
Pluto was as cold as an icebox
Saturn, Jupiter, Venus and Mars
The story I've told you think isn't true
To me it is you must understand.

*Scott Franklin (10)*
*The Moat Junior School*


## A WORLD

A world full of hate and greed,
Famine, foe and nothing to feed.

So why do people stand and stare?
Soon it'll be gone, nothing there.

Wicked people with a child's cry,
Tears drop while eagles fly.

A world full of hate and greed,
Famine, foe and nothing to feed.

*Ben Hooper (9)*
*The Moat Junior School*

## Owls

Owls have perfect eyes
they can see crystal clear

They have beautiful, silky wings
like two rafts being smashed against each other

Their talons are enormous and sharp
like rats' teeth

They can fly off a tree swooping
they dig their talons into a mouse
like a crane grabbing a plank of metal

Then they peck into the mouse
like a can of Coke spilling over a table

Then the sun comes up
owls are sleeping like a log.

*Sean Johnson (10)*
*The Moat Junior School*


## Spiders

I hate creepy-crawlies -
They go everywhere!
When you break their webs
To clean the window
They're still there.
They're smudging on your window
And getting in your way -
But when you get them down again,
They'll keep coming back.

*Michelle Blackford (8)*
*The Moat Junior School*

## SCHOOL LIFE

I wish I could see
What school holds for me

I like to run around
In our big playground
My teacher is great

She helps us create
The dinners I enjoy
I wish we could take toys.

*Michael MacDonald (9)*
*The Moat Junior School*

## THE TIGER

T he forest is the tiger's home
I t is a bit of a scary animal
G o and visit it if you dare
E ating is very hard in the forest because someone's bound to stare
R ains most of the time in the forest.

*Anne Carpenter (8)*
*The Moat Junior School*

## MY DAD'S TOOLS

My dad's tools are really sharp.
My dad's tools can be thrown like a dart.
My dad's tools can cut down a tree.
My dad's tools are too dangerous for me.

*Josh Patel (10)*
*The Moat Junior School*

# I Wonder

I sit in bed wondering what it must be like,
wrapped up in bandages really tight,
with metal staples in my head,
stuck in a wheelchair not being able to move and hardly being fed.

I wonder what it must be like,
to lie in bed and see no daylight,
children with no food to eat,
I'll sure they'll want a piece of meat.

I wonder what it must be like,
for people in wars must be hard,
to be rationed over fruit and veg,
or even losing a leg.

I wonder what it must be like,
for children with problems or something's not right.

I wonder, I wonder
what it must be
like.

*Karina Clutterbuck (10)*
*The Moat Junior School*


# Animals

A   nimals are cute,
N   obody likes the smell of skunks,
I    like hamsters best of all,
M   ammoths are big,
A   nd I like horses,
L   ambs are baby sheep,
S   ometimes I see foxes in my garden.

*Daniel Vijay (9)*
*The Moat Junior School*

## THE BATTLE

Gold, sharp, shafts of Rama's magic arrows,
Dug into the demon's horrific figures,
Blood lusted devils retaliated in full force,
Sudden panic erupted among the monkeys

Crashing through glass,
Clear as crystal,
Rama unleashed the destructive arrow with speed of a bullet,
Ravana falls, as darkness pulls him down.

*Sam Vijay (10)*
*The Moat Junior School*


## ME-MOVING

I swim, I swing
I dance, I dash
I cry, crawl and creep
I run, I ride
I skip, I skid
And frequently I smile.

I step, I stride
I glue, I glide
I skid, I ski
I turn, I trip and try
I play, I pay
I jump, I jive
And now and then
I wonder why.

*Michaela Marsh (9)*
*The Moat Junior School*

## RABBITS

Cute and cuddly, fluffy and round,
they can't live in the sea, so they live on the ground.
Rabbits eat grass, pellets, vegetables and sometimes hay,
they like lots of love and care but they also like to play.
They come in all colours - grey, brown, black and white,
they look gentle and soppy, but they sometimes bite.
Rabbits live in burrows, or in a hutch,
they don't like dirty homes very much.
Baby rabbits grow strong and tall,
I like them best when they're cute and small!

*Natasha Ogden (9)*
*The Moat Junior School*


## ME-MOVING

I jig and jump
I slip and slide
I splash and spin
I scamper, skate and scramble
I stamp and stomp
I chomp and chip
And frequently, I gambol

I leap and lurch
I skip and skid
I strut and stride
I rave, romp and rumble
I turn and trip
I dart and dash
I skid and slip
And now and then, I tumble.

*Jordan Bombera (8)*
*The Moat Junior School*

## THE WEATHER

What is thunder?
Two very angry clouds fighting in the sky.

Why does it rain?
So you can get the evil out of us.

What is fog?
When the clouds blow down on earth.

What is the sun?
A strong beaming light that won't let enemies into Heaven.

*Larissa Woodhouse (10)*
*The Moat Junior School*


## MY AGE

When I was one, I sucked my thumb
When I was two, I started to glue
When I was three, I was a flea
When I was four, I kicked the door
When I was five, I learned to dive
When I was six, I learned to mix
When I was seven, I could count to eleven
When I was eight, I went on a date
When I was nine, I liked Calvin Klein
When I was ten, I met Ken.

*Joanna Alice Clarke (8)*
*The Moat Junior School*

## NIGHT

It was late when I woke from a very bad dream,
And although it was quiet, it did not seem -
That I was alone in my room!
As I trembled, the curtains did loom,
And I reached for Ted,
But he was not in my bed!

I went to my sister and turned on her light,
She squinted it was so bright.
'Sis, you know the 'thing' under my bed,
That 'thing' - it's taken Ted!'
'It's probably fallen out,' she told me.
'Just look, you'll see.'

Suddenly I remembered where I'd left Ted,
I had left him in the shed!
He would protect me from the 'terrible thing',
Under my bed with its claws and its wings.
So, out in the night I crept,
Over the wet grass I leapt,
While bats flew over me,
And bears in the bushes waited hungrily.
I reached the shed door,
Trod over the cobwebbed floor,
Felt dust and mothy wings,
And other such things,
Until . . . at last, I found Ted,
And went back to bed.
(I had forgotten the 'thing'!)

*Dominic Lane (8)*
*The Richard Pate School*

## NIGHT

I'm in bed and I'm getting very scared.
Strange noises everywhere, creaking of the radiators.
My night-light isn't working; there are shapes on the wall.
I can't switch on my light because there are scorpions on the floor.
I know I can't shout for Mum and Dad,
I can't reach the door.

Perhaps if I sing to cheer myself up to make me brave
And cuddle up to Huggy Bear and pray,
Between the three of us, God, my bear and me,
We can make the spookies go away.

What was that? I was nearly asleep!
A shiver runs up my spine.
There's a squeak, click and scratching sound,
The bedroom door comes ajar.
Mum whispers 'Are you asleep yet?'
My eyes tightly shut and a pretend little snore.
She quietly shuts the door.

*Michael Greene (9)*
*The Richard Pate School*


## THE NIGHT I WAS SCARED

One night I told my mum not to turn out the light.
At midnight I woke with a fright,
I turned around and there was nothing much to see,
But one old picture and a hanging bumblebee.

I took one glimpse at the clock,
1am I thought tick-tock, tick-tock.
I saw a shadow on the stairs,
I thought it was a group of bears.

I saw something on the landing floor,
I peeped around my bedroom door.
I thought it was the bogeyman's skin,
'Nah!' I said and put it in the bin.

When I crept back up the stairs,
All I saw was the group of bears.
I got back into bed and wrapped up tight
And all I said was goodnight.

***Charlotte Morton (9)***
***The Richard Pate School***


# NIGHT

Crash! Bang! Wallop! Middle of the night.
Something gave me a horrible fright.
It must be the trees, put on the light.
Oh, it's only the curtains blowing in the breeze.

When the shadows come out.
The ghosts begin to shout.
Will the bogeyman go away? I'll pray.

To stop me getting such a fright.
I think I'll get a night-light.
When I start to shake and quiver.
It makes me want to shiver.

Foxes going through the bins.
Are eating all the tins.
What's the time?
Did you hear that chime?

There's something under my bed.
I hope it's only a ted.

***Imogen Ryley (9)***
***The Richard Pate School***

## NIGHT

At night I heard a scary noise,
But what is it?
Mum said I was dreaming it,
So I went back to bed
And cuddled my ted.
I thought I heard something under my bed.

I thought it was a big blob,
So I let out a sob
And Daddy came into my room,
'There's a scary blob under my bed'
But when we looked it was gone.
I thought I heard something under my bed.

I put on my dressing gown
And went onto the dark landing,
Past all my toys
And my model island.
I couldn't see the scary blob,
But I'm sure I heard something under my bed.

*Jack Sim (8)*
*The Richard Pate School*


## NIGHT

One night I thought I heard a scream,
I said 'Oh silly me it must have been a dream,'
I definitely heard some creaking coming from the stair,
I'm sure I saw a shape give me a terrible glare.

I snuggled down in my quilt holding my favourite teddy bear,
Trying not to face the door, in case he appeared there,
I called my mum but no reply,
All I heard was a groaning sigh.

Then at last my mum appeared,
At first I thought she was someone weird,
'Now settle down my little child,
You let your imagination run wild.

Just because it's dark at night,
It doesn't mean the bogeyman will give you a fright!
So close your eyes and count sheep,
Before you know it, you will be fast asleep.'

*Shona Pratt (8)*
*The Richard Pate School*


# NIGHT

Night is so creepy, spooky and all,
Lots of shadows begin to grow tall.
When the bogeyman starts to quiver,
I get a funny feeling in my liver.

Soon the doors blow and creak,
Then I really want to shriek.
When my mum comes to turn off the light,
I imagine a terrible sight.

Asleep in my bed facing the wall,
If I turn around the bogeyman might call.
Outside the house there's a noise in the trees,
I jumped out of bed and fell on my knees.

There I stayed cold on the floor,
Scared that something might come through the door.
I waited until I saw morning was near,
Then I knew there was nothing to fear.

*Amanda Ripley (8)*
*The Richard Pate School*

## NIGHT

I don't like the night at all,
When I see lots of shadows on the wall,
It makes me shake and quiver,
It looks like a ghost and I start to shiver.
Then snuggled up in my bed,
I cuddle up tight with my ted.
I hear a creak on the stair,
I wonder if the monster could be there.
He has wings like a bat and his eyes are bright red,
He looks like he came from the land of the dead.
Then I hear a faint scream,
I wake up and find it was all a dream.

*Francesca White (8)*
*The Richard Pate School*


## NIGHT

It was quiet in the house,
Until I heard a bark,
I crept out of bed to fetch my torch
And wandered in the dark.

I tiptoed down the creaking stairs,
In my dressing gown,
I searched around the house,
But nothing could be found.

I ran outside
And saw a burglar with a dog,
I called the police,
Who arrived in the fog.

*David Hackett (8)*
*The Richard Pate School*

## NIGHT

I always sleep facing the door,
The night-light on and the dark blue floor,
I quiver with fear when the shadows come near,
I think it's a frail man to take me from here.

I always sleep facing the door,
The bogeyman shrinks and slithers along the floor,
The scary noises silently creak,
I see the bogeyman open his beak.

I always sleep facing the door,
In case a zombie comes in or something raw,
The cuts on my arm look so sore,
So that is why I sleep facing the door.

*Harry Young (9)*
*The Richard Pate School*


## NIGHT

One night,
I had a real fright,
I poked my leg out of my bed,
Held on to my ted.

This bogeyman came out from under my bed
And he actually took my favourite ted.
I saw the moving of his knees,
But it was only the shadows of the trees.

I always face the door,
Not the floor,
As I lie in my bed,
I dream of things in my head.

*Emily Field (8)*
*The Richard Pate School*

## NIGHT

It all started when I was alone in the dark,
When a dog gave a quivering bark.

I was scared and screamed loudly,
I felt alone and very cowardly.

I saw these yellow eyes under my bed,
They looked as though they were in the back of its head.

Someone came up the stairs
And gave me these terrible glares.

I hid waiting for him to disappear
And trembled with thundering fear.

It's singing a song,
Which sounds very wrong.

I wish he would go away, he is driving me mad,
Oh, it's only Dad!

*Amelia Peace (8)*
*The Richard Pate School*


## THE MAN UNDER MY BED

It's always at night there's a man under my bed,
'He isn't there!' my mummy said.
But he is always there with a very big gun,
He tortures me, he thinks it's good fun!
But he's always there, the man under my bed.

He's squat and stubby with a missing toe,
With red eyes that glow.
There's a man under my bed,
With my ted,
But he's always there, the man under my bed.

He sneaks around in a thick floating black cloak,
He's creeping behind me he'll give me a hurtful poke.
'He isn't there' my daddy said,
*But he is* there, I promise, I swear,
 The man under my bed . . .

*Hannah Barraclough (8)*
*The Richard Pate School*


## MY LANE

One fine morning I was walking down my country lane
When I looked up I saw the blue sky
When I looked down
I saw my dog.
I could hear the birds singing in the trees while they were rustling
And the dogs barking at the birds
Scared them away
From their nests
I just carried on walking
Down my country lane
I was halfway down
I saw an old lady
'Hi' I said
And no reply from her.
I saw my house from here
But I had to cross the deadly road
I heard the sounds of the cars
I quickly did a runner past the cars
Now all I had to do was
Open
The gate.

*Tim Pettitt (8)*
*Tewkesbury CE Primary School*

## WHY, HOW, WHAT, WHERE?

How can people walk and talk?
How can lions roar?
Why do bears roar so loud?
Why do gorillas speak so funny?
Why do monkeys swing on trees?
How can birds fly so high?
How can fish swim so deep?
How can kangaroos jump so high?
Why do elephants have long trunks?
Why do dogs growl and howl?
Why do bees sting when they are angry?
How can spiders walk into our houses?
How can the sun shine so bright?

*Lucy Paginton (9)*
*Tewkesbury CE Primary School*


## WHY?

Why do animals catch their prey?
Why do birds fly?
Why do bees sting?
Why do builders build houses?
Why do grown-ups work?
Why don't children go to work?
Why are elephants so big?
Why are ants so small?
Why do fish go in water?
Where does food come from?
What would happen if we had none left?

*Emma King (10)*
*Tewkesbury CE Primary School*

## HOW DO BIRDS FLY?

How do birds fly?
Why am I a girl?
How does the world go round?
How does it turn day and night?
Why does it rain?
How do the clouds move?
How does the grass grow?
Why do we talk?
How do we swim?
How do we grow old?
Why do we have hair?
How do people talk different languages?
How do we move?
How do plants grow?
How do we eat?
How do fish eat?
Why are people horrible?
How do the stars come out?

*Shardai Thomas (9)*
*Tewkesbury CE Primary School*


## WHY? WHY?

Why am I a boy?
Why do I break my toys?
How can I kick a ball?
Why do we sit on the floor?
Why do we have a house?
Why does rain fall from the sky?
Why do we go to school?

*Daniel Defty (10)*
*Tewkesbury CE Primary School*

## COUNTRY LANE

I was walking down a lane,
A very narrow lane.
I was happy but sad,
My friends would not walk with me
But I was all right because it was snowing.
It was dark,
Dark and gloomy.
There were animals running all over the place,
There were young kids, old kids and adults.
It was getting even darker.
There were three storey buildings.
There was an owl hooting.
I was getting scared,
I started to run.
The wind was howling,
I was still running.
Finally I had reached my house,
My house, my things, my family.
I was home,
I was safe.

*Jessica Courtney (10)*
*Tewkesbury CE Primary School*

## DOWN THE LANE

One fine summer afternoon
I decided to go for a walk down the lane,
The lane was wide and straight.
I went down a bit further,
I heard stones crunching under my feet.
Then I met a lady with her dog.
There were gigantic walls
With green plants over it,
It made the lane look stunning.

All I could hear was the trees rattling side to side.
It was really nice, I had a happy feeling,
I was wearing white trainers with a cap.
I walked on, I came to a gate,
I went through, there were flowers,
I went back home.

*Kelly Wynne (8)*
*Tewkesbury CE Primary School*

# W

What eats the wind?
Why do we have bins?
Why do we have the world a mess?
Why do we have homes?
Why don't we live on the streets?
Why do we have pets?
Why don't they live in the wild?
Why do ladies have babies?
Why do we have food?
Why are rabbits pests to farmers?
Why do we have guns?
Why did Hitler start a war?
Why do foxes eat meat?
Why do people destroy buildings?
Why do people hate others?
Why do we have TVs?
What do people hate the most?
Why do we have schools?
Why do we have games?
Why do most girls hate mice?
Why do people live on the streets?

*Ben Torr (10)*
*Tewkesbury CE Primary School*

## WHY?

Why do we have the
moon and sun?
Why do we have
wind and rain?
Why is the sun
so hot?
Why do we have
rivers that flow?
Why do trees
sway in the wind?
Why do we have
days of the week?
Why do we have
birds that sing?
Why do we have
cows, sheep and pigs?

*Gemma Newman (10)*
*Tewkesbury CE Primary School*

## DOWN MY LANE

I was walking down the lane,
Not a cloud in sight.
The sun shining in my eyes,
I see a summer walk,
I see a lot of people
On the summer walk.
I am very hot,
So I am sweating.
I suddenly look at the time,
It is 5:00.
I hear my mum calling.

*Sam Cotton (8)*
*Tewkesbury CE Primary School*

## WHY? HOW? QUESTIONS

Why does a cat chase a mouse?
How does a builder build a brick house?

Why does a tortoise move so slowly?
How does the wind blow so strongly?

Why don't snails like sunny weather?
Why don't cats and dogs get on together?

How does a monkey swing from tree to tree?
Why do people sometimes sneeze?

Why did Britain and Germany go to war?
Why do criminals break the law?

Why do people talk so loud?
How does God make a cloud?

Why do people have a bath?
How does a clown make us laugh?

*Fahad Nazmul (9)*
*Tewkesbury CE Primary School*


## A WALK IN THE COUNTRYSIDE

I was walking in a new lane
And life was all round me.
It was very steep and sloping down
And a very long way down.
Birds were chuckling
Green mountains in the background.
I was wearing sneakers.
The lane was very dry but . . .
At the end of the lane was a flood.

*Jamie Powell (8)*
*Tewkesbury CE Primary School*

## UP AT THE LIGHTHOUSE

I was walking up the lighthouse in Ireland,
It was freezing cold, it was snowing,
I really like going for a walk on Boxing Day,
I could hear the dark blue sea splash against the rocks,
There were people whistling up the lighthouse,
I saw two lovely houses they were massive,
My grandad was telling us about the caves,
Friendly people saying hello,
I thought we were nearly there
I went around the corner
And saw about fifty steps,
We were nearly there,
It was beautiful
I was exhausted,
The sea smelt fishy
But I enjoyed it.

*Charlotte Hamilton (10)*
*Tewkesbury CE Primary School*


## WALKING DOWN A COUNTRY LANE

One day I was walking down a country lane
That had bushes on either side
It was a summer day
All I could hear were
Birds, planes and some cars.
As I went on
I saw some flower beds
I began to run with my dog
I slowed down at a house
It was my friend.

*Sam Devine (9)*
*Tewkesbury CE Primary School*

## DOWN MY LANE

The season is autumn down my lane,
Cloudy and cold and falling rain.
The lane is twisting, winding and narrow
And overhead I see an occasional sparrow.
The sides are covered with trees and bushes
And I also see a man who rushes.
A hare darts across in front of me,
I fish in my pocket for a key.
I'm nearly home now, where it is cosy and warm,
My dad's in the back somewhere, mowing the lawn.
I open the front door, call out 'Hi!'
My brother, he's a meanie, he just said: 'Bye!'
So that's the end of my walk now,
I must take a bow,
I have to go anyway,
So I'll go on my way.

*Stacey Baldwin (8)*
*Tewkesbury CE Primary School*


## THE STREET

A busy street I walked through swishing side to side
It's the middle of winter, freezing cold.
I was going to the shops but I went to Burger King instead.
The road was narrow and sharp.
Many birds had gone but a few stayed behind
It just smelled like chips.
People older than me walked by
I heard people and cars in the windy weather.
People rushing into bright shops
When I was feeling cold in the winter's wind.

*Christopher Callow (9)*
*Tewkesbury CE Primary School*

## A Naughty Little Scene

I was walking,
I was walking down a cobbled street.
The wind was winding its way through the air,
It whistled in the keyholes. In places it is colourful,
In other places it is dark colours.
There were big dark brick walls on either side,
With flower beds at the bottom.
I started walking.
As I walked slowly down the street,
The wind beat fiercely against my face.
The leaves are gone,
Where are they now?
In the distance I can see a train crossing,
I looked up to see a big hill with a dog chasing the sheep.
I could hear birds as they flew over in a V shape.
I was wearing trainers,
The lane was very bumpy.
It was a clear day so I could see far.
Then I stopped.
There is a gate,
A criss-cross gate.
There is a sign,
It says *Private Property*.
I nudged the gate,
A car alarm went off!
Before I knew it I was racing back up the street.

*Callum Kerr (8)*
*Tewkesbury CE Primary School*

## MY WINTER WALK

It's winter and bitterly cold,
I'm walking down a narrow lane
Ice cracks when I walk.
My feet are numb.
I see an old lady walk past with her dog,
She's bitterly cold too.
I hear cars skidding on the ice
It makes a screeching noise
And frightens the little dog with the old lady.
I'm surrounded by big black walls.
The air smells damp and wet
And when I look up I see grey sky
With birds flying in line.
I'm wrapped up warm.
I'm wearing my new trainers,
My scarf, hat, gloves,
My new HM high mound coat.
I'm on my way home now.
I walk past a dark alley.
I'm just walking into my house.
It's warm and my dad's sat in the chair
Reading the newspaper.
My mum's laid down on the sofa watching TV.
My sister's upstairs reading.
I'm taking my coat, gloves, hat and shoes off.
I go and sit with my mum
And tell her about the walk.

*Abigail Bullingham (9)*
*Tewkesbury CE Primary School*

## ONE FINE SUNNY DAY

I was walking
Down the street feeling down
Because it was a fine sunny day
And it was Christmas Day and
Nobody was playing outside with me
It had just been World War III
There were no children out
I was surrounded by trees
People were wailing from the pain
No beautiful smells of Christmas puddings
There was pounding weather
Like a sledgehammer hitting a building
There was also no traffic around
Just smudges of blood over houses
And wails.

*Lee Phillips (9)*
*Tewkesbury CE Primary School*


## DOWN MY LANE

The season was summer
And I was walking down a thin and narrow lane.
Either side of me was a pond
With ducks in it
The birds were singing in the background
The sky was full of glitter.
I was alone
Wearing boots and thin trousers.
There were rabbits eating carrots by the river
At dinner it smelt of curry.

*Rebecca Ricketts (8)*
*Tewkesbury CE Primary School*

## IN THE COUNTRYSIDE

It was late summer
And my hands were getting number.
It was too cold for me,
My friend's name is Lee.
The lane was winding and narrow,
I saw a couple of sparrows.
Around me I saw lots of meadows with golden crops,
But there weren't any shops.
I heard a squirrel cracking a nut
And then woodpeckers going tut, tut.
Under my feet the mud was squelching,
I was wearing boots that were easy to crouch in.
Far away I saw flowers and trees
And berries, also a few bees.
It wasn't very hot but it was very blowy.
I felt very sweaty, although it was really snowy.
There were lots of colours like red and blue
And a bit of green and a colour like glue.

*Rebecca Nash (8)*
*Tewkesbury CE Primary School*


## MY STREET

My street has no life
Except for a man with his wife
My street has a blue sky
And there's a river running by
In my street there's lots of caravan parks
Where the street ends and the country starts
My street has a brown countryside
People by the boat waiting for a ride.

*William Devine (10)*
*Tewkesbury CE Primary School*

## GOING HOME

I was walking down the street,
All around, whispering and mumbling,
Autumn leaves all soggy and brown,
Tripping and stumbling.
Big whiskery cats,
On my way home,
People taller than giants,
Little children walking alone.
Hailstones as big as footballs,
Car horns screech,
Police cars whine,
Cigarette smoke,
People doing time.
Walking down my road,
My house in sight,
Up to my warm bed,
To sleep for the night.

*Rachel Gibbs (10)*
*Tewkesbury CE Primary School*


## DOWN THE COUNTRY LANE

One summer's day I was walking down a country lane,
There were a lot of trees, bins and bushes,
There was so much sandy mud
It was right up to my knees,
There was a farm on the left and a field on the right,
It was boiling hot,
I was riding my horse and so was my dog,
I saw a gate
It was the gate for the end of the lane
Goodbye.

*Emily Blackwell (8)*
*Tewkesbury CE Primary School*

## SPRING WALK

The season is spring
And all that happens in spring is:
Rain, rain, rain and more rain.
The trainers in which I walk are soaked and full of:
Mud, mud, mud and more mud.
The path twists and turns,
The lane itself is:
Rough, rough and rougher.
Fields are gooey,
Lightning:
Flashes, flashes, flashes and flashes more.
Distant thunder rumbles
And everything is:
Miserable, miserable, miserable and more miserable.
The good thing about it is the wonderful colours of:
Crisp brown leaves, the soaked green grass of the field.
The loneliness of the lane,
Makes it seem like mine.
I love my lane,
Pity about the weather though.

*John Vincent (9)*
*Tewkesbury CE Primary School*


## ON MY WALK I SAW ...

S oaking wet boys and girls
U nder the water we go cooling down
M ums sunbathing
M ost people scorching
E ating, smelling barbecues
R aging hot mums and dads.

*Chris Tarling (9)*
*Tewkesbury CE Primary School*

## THE STREET

Once I was walking down a long, wide street,
With my short, tired feet.
Loads of cars passing by and parking each side,
Luckily they don't collide!
Birds chirping high above,
On the path, there's a glove.
Usually it spits with rain,
But in the car park there's a big drain.
There's people sitting on the wall,
With their big soccer ball.
Usually there's a smoky smell,
Which makes the street smell like Hell.
There's rubbish on the side of the wall,
Because there's always a big stall.
Big flats and little houses,
Which always make little noises.
Trees on both sides at the end
And there's more round the bend.

*Rhys Bestwick (9)*
*Tewkesbury CE Primary School*


## IN THE COUNTRYSIDE

In the countryside I can see:

People talking,
Children walking,
New people looking around.

In the countryside I can hear:

Animals scratching,
Children screaming,
Parents arguing,
Babies crying.

In the countryside I can smell:

Fires burning,
Hot dogs just coming off the stove
And last of all the breeze.

In the countryside I can feel:

Grass that's wet,
Animals that are soft
And hot dogs that have just gone in my mouth.

*Rebecca Ramplin (9)*
*Tewkesbury CE Primary School*


## COUNTRY LANE POEM

It's a hot day in a wide back lane,
I'm playing in a field to ease away that horrid pain.
Exploring around and guess what I found,
I found a huge and smelly hay mound.
Climbing up step by step soon to reach the top,
Finding ahead of me a ragged old mop.
Climbing back down again I take a slip,
Almost breaking my fingertip.
When then I saw my friend Andrew,
At the same time all the cows went *moo!*
When we heard some new birds around,
We decided to leave a nest on the mound.
Waiting behind for something to come,
All day long nothing was done.
As we left we smelt a fire,
Nothing we saw but a quagmire.

*Ian Vedmore (10)*
*Tewkesbury CE Primary School*

## WALKING DOWN A COUNTRY LANE

Walking down a country lane,
To ease away that awful pain.
Birds are flying overhead,
Singing on their way to bed.

The awful pain it is so bad,
It makes me feel really sad.
The pain is of the horrid spring term,
Or could it be a horrid germ?

A squirrel leaping from tree to tree,
There's something else what could it be?
Oh no, please help, it is my mum,
I think I'm gonna have to run!

You see, I have been missing school,
Instead I lie where it is cool.
I listen to the animals,
While playing with my bouncy ball.

Too late! I'm caught, I say goodbye,
To all the squirrels and birds that fly.
I am now stuck in my room,
Watching the eclipse of the moon.

*Ashleigh Hesslewood (10)*
*Tewkesbury CE Primary School*

## THE LANE

The lane was noisy,
People talking about houses,
Green trees blocking the light,
There was no end at all it kept going on and on,
People shouting and screaming for light.
The lane had cats, dogs and birds making loads of noise,
There was a little blue shop with loads of food,
A mother and a baby,
The mother, thirteen and the baby, two months old,
The father, fifteen, they were stealing.
There are no houses, they live in the lane.
A little boy in pain,
Screaming for help,
A boy called William started to walk with me,
I was scared about never coming out.

*Georgina Harvey (10)*
*Tewkesbury CE Primary School*


## THE SHIPWRECK

Abandoned alone in the stormy seas,
With nothing else to do,
Apart from watching the storming waves,
As high as the clouds, as loud as thunder,
Yet, somehow, like candytufts flowering white, pink and blue.
Getting closer to the rocks, I'm getting very scared.
When will be the crunch,
Not now, not now, *now!*
Ouch, yow, that water's cold.
All alone on the rocks,
Waves getting higher,
*Help me!*

*Charlotte Sherwood (8)*
*Toddington Primary School*

## WATER

The waves chewed hastily at the rocks
As the waves got impatient
They begin to rise with no manners
They ate the boats and discarded their bones.

They lay back ready to pounce
Like a big cat
The waves dashed up to the shore
With not a care in the world.

They grew bigger and bigger and stronger
As they grew they lost respect
The waves slammed theirselves
Onto their frightened prey.

Their prey was scared and frightened
As the predator laughed with glee
It came to an end
But still with no respect.

*Paula Thomas (10)*
*Tuffley Primary School*


## SPOTTY DOG

One day my dream will be,
To have a special friend just for me.
I imagine it to be a big white dog
With shiny black spots.
Every day when he comes to get me out of bed,
He'll lick me.
'Spotty, Spotty, you lovely dog.'
Every day we will play together,
We will love each other forever.

*Stacey Davis (11)*
*Tuffley Primary School*

## FOOD POEM

I went to the shops,
To buy for my tea,
Six sizzling sausages,
Yummy for me.

I went to the shops,
To buy for my breakfast,
Big bacon butty,
Which I ate with mustard.

I went to the shops,
To buy for my lunch,
Brilliant baked beans,
I went munch, munch.

I went to the shops,
To buy for my supper,
Nice Nik-Nak nuggets,
Which I ate with garlic butter.

***Daniel Anderson (9)***
***Tuffley Primary School***


## DOWN BY THE SWAMP

Down by the swamp,
On a very sunny day,
See the leaping lion,
Catching his prey.

Down by the swamp,
Hear the lion roar,
See the leaping lion,
Jumping to the floor.

***Daniel Brookes (8)***
***Tuffley Primary School***

## BABIES

I hate babies,
They drive me up the wall,
They cry at anything
I don't like them at all!

They throw food at me
And scream all night
In the morning
I wake up such a sight!

They can be all right
But not all the time
They scream and shout
And bawl and whine.

I kinda like babies
When they grow,
Will I have one?
I don't think so!

*Jade Ryan (10)*
*Tuffley Primary School*


## SPORTS

S occer games are lots of fun,
P laying them with everyone.
O ver the bar lots of cheer,
R ugby is the game of the year.
T ime to go and get a shower,
S o I'll be ready for football in an hour.

*Eddie Carter (9)*
*Tuffley Primary School*

## SYDNEY

The bridge where people climb,
Opera singers sing aloud,
The mistaken capital,
Olympic stadium, home of rugby,
Harbour's big where ships lay,
Canberra's the quickest route,
Oldest settlement in Aussie land.

Have you guessed yet?

*Sydney.*

**Leigh Dangerfield (11)**
**Tuffley Primary School**


## ALL WE NEED

Food in our tummies
Hats on our heads
Water to quench us
Sheets on our beds.

Teachers to teach us
Shoes on our feet
Trousers and T-shirt
Shelter and heat.

Someone to love us
Someone to love
Hope for the future
Light from above.

**Leah Davis (10)**
**Tuffley Primary School**

## STORM

As the black clouds gather
They look like lions ready to pounce
On the innocent village
Rain taps against the timid rooftops.

Suddenly a flood of rain comes crashing down
On the petrified village
A strike of lightning
Tortures the tumbling trees
The thunder teases the terrified village.

*King Yip (11)*
*Tuffley Primary School*


## FRIENDS

I have lots of friends
On which I can depend
They all really like me
Sometimes they come to tea

I play with my friends every day
But sometimes they don't come out to play
I have a best friend called Yasmin
We both sing and make an awful din

    But there again she's my best friend
        And on her I can depend!

*Laura Barnard (10)*
*Tuffley Primary School*

## THUNDER

Thunder claps at the trees
It laughs as the trees dodge its sting
Trees get dazzled by a bright flash
Thunder goes for the kill but misses its target
The thunder frowns but the trees just giggle
Thunder shouts at the trees, they start to cry
Then thunder goes for the chop
And the trees scream as they fall.

*Shaun Beresford (11)*
*Tuffley Primary School*


## WATER

Water crashes out of the iron tap
Against the aluminium sink.
The water fills a glass halfway by itself,
Water slides happily down the throat,
Trying to find the blood stream.

*Natalie Beard (10)*
*Tuffley Primary School*


## EGYPT

Pyramids so high,
Mount to the sky.
As the soft sand blows,
The bright sun glows.
I approach the tomb,
I reach my doom.
In the dark, dull, cursed room.

*Kerry Brookes (11)*
*Tuffley Primary School*

## HEARD IT IN THE CLASSROOM

Heard
Heard it
Heard it in
Heard it in the
Heard it in the class
Heard it in the classroom

The classroom
The classroom
The class
The class
The classroom
The classroom
The class
The class

Heard it in the classroom
Scribble, scribble
Heard it in the classroom
Pass me the rubber
The rubber
The rubber
Heard it in the classroom
I broke my pencil
My pencil
My pencil

Heard it in the classroom
Be quiet please, please
I've got a headache
A headache
A headache

Heard it in the *classroom!*

*Jake Dabbs (10)*
*Tuffley Primary School*

## JOURNEY ON A TRAIN

At a wink of the eye,
The station goes by,
All in a blur of colour.
Birds and bees
Fly through trees,
Animals diving for cover.

It starts to rain,
There's an aeroplane,
Fly by in a car.
It starts to get cold,
As the hills start to fold
And I need something warmer to wear.

Squirrels scurry,
They're all in a hurry,
Running up trees in a flash.
Hail starts to fall,
Pitter-patter on a wall,
Streams go by in a dash.

Station draws nearer,
Sky's getting clearer,
Train's getting closer to home.
I'll soon be at my house,
Where I'll see my pet mouse,
Now Mum isn't alone.

*Katherine Anderson (11)*
*Tuffley Primary School*